A Taste of Catholicism II

A New Generation

A Taste of Catholicism II
A New Generation

Cathedral Foundation Press
Baltimore, Maryland

Printed and bound in the United States of America.

1 2 3 4 5   05 04 03 02 01 00 99 98 97 96

Library of Congress Catalog Card Number: 96-85748

ISBN 1-885938-10-1

Published in 1997 by

 Cathedral Foundation Press
P.O. Box 777
Baltimore, Maryland 21203

Publisher: Daniel L. Medinger
Assistant Manager: Patti Medinger
Design & Illustration: Francis Koerber
Cover photograph: Ann Curtin
Production Assistant: Lisa Wiseman

Contents

ntroduction

When preparing the introduction for A TASTE OF
CATHOLICISM, RECIPES FOR THE BODY AND
SOUL, the idea of publishing a first-ever archdiocesan
cookbook was very exciting and overwhelming. Now
a year later Cathedral Foundation Press is savoring
the sweet smells of success and are eager to launch an
all new second edition, A TASTE OF CATHOLICISM
II, A NEW GENERATION.

A special thanks to all our cooks who contributed
their recipes and generously shared family memories
and traditions. Our focus for this cookbook was to
provide recipes for a new generation of health
conscious eaters, and offer variety and good taste. We
are happy to tell you that your palates will be
pleasantly pleased. The recipes we received were of
varied tastes, and will give you many choices
including totally fat free meals. The American Heart
Association graciously has provided a wide variety of
low-fat and low cholesterol recipes including
marvelous main dishes to dramatic desserts. For your
convenience we have put all these recipes in a special
section called, "Heart Smart." These delicacies are not
only delicious, but good for you too! Take a minute
and think about a mouth watering meal beginning
with a Lemon Waldorf Salad, followed by Braised
Sirloin Tips, Stuffed Acorn Squash, Yogurt Dinner
Rolls and for the grand finale....Baked Ginger Pears.

Yumm! All these recipes and many more can be found in our new and exciting cookbook...A TASTE OF CATHOLICISM II, A NEW GENERATION.

A special congratulations to Ann Curtin from St. Mary's Parish in Annapolis for submitting the winning photo of her daughter Laura, which appears on the front cover. The four year old seems to have captured not only a huge Maryland blue crab, but shows the picture perfect richness of a new generation carrying on old traditions. Bravo! Read more tidbits about Ann Curtin and her fond memories of family and food while growing up in Baltimore, following the introduction.

A TASTE OF CATHOLICISM II, A NEW GENERATION is a book that is truly good enough to eat....but we recommend buying more than one copy. Treat yourself and surprise a friend with his or her own TASTE OF CATHOLICISM II. Bon Appetite!

Patti Medinger
Editor

Cover Photo

A MEMORY

by Ann Curtin, St. Mary's Parish, Annapolis

*I*have many fond memories of growing up in Baltimore in the late *1960's - most of them involving food and family. In my childhood the two were always linked. Besides our own family picnics* (featuring my mother's famous shrimp dip!) *there were the annual Catholic War Veteran Picnics, the spaghetti dinners at church and eating hot dogs at Memorial Stadium. I remember we were even allowed to drink a Coke while cheering on the O's. I'll never forget hunting for Easter eggs or the way our own house smelled when my mom prepared Thanksgiving dinner with all the trimmings.*

There is no food in the world, however, better than the Maryland blue crab. If I have to think of one food synonymous with my Baltimore childhood it would be steamed crabs. Summer was just not summer without

crabs. Of course, we ventured out, with varying degrees of success to catch our own, but the best times were when my father would surprise us by bringing them home with him after work. He would always bring them in a plain brown bag. The tips of their sharp claws and shells poking out through tiny holes. We knew from experience not to grab that bag because - ouch!....you might get a cut that the Old Bay seasoning would bother all night long.

I'm grown up now and I moved down to Annapolis, but summer is still not summer without crabs. I'd like to submit these pictures of my own "little crabber," my daughter Laura, who at four years old can dip a crab with such precision and speed that there can be no doubt that she was born in Maryland.

A Taste of Catholicism

II

A New Generation

Beverages

Frosty Cappuccino

Aileen Sohn, Baltimore

1/4 cup ground coffee
2 teaspoons grated orange rind
2 teaspoons cocoa
1/4 teaspoon ground cinnamon
1-3/4 cups water
1 cup skim milk
1/3 cup firmly packed brown sugar
2 tablespoons coffee liqueur

Combine grounds and orange rind in coffee filter or filter basket of a drip coffeemaker. Place cocoa and cinnamon in coffeepot. Add 1-3/4 cups water to coffeemaker. Prepare according to instructions. Stir in milk and remaining ingredients. Pour into a shallow container; freeze until firm. Break frozen mixture into chunks. Process in a blender or processor until smooth.

Cranberry Delight

Aileen Sohn, Baltimore

2 (12 ounce cans) frozen cranberry juice concentrate, thawed and undiluted
2 (33.8 ounce bottles) ginger ale, chilled

Combine ingredients and serve chilled over crushed ice or fruit-flavored ice cubes. Makes 2-3/4 quarts.

Energy Drink

Patti Medinger, Church of Nativity, Timonium

1-2 cups of skim milk (may substitute non-fat yogurt)
1 banana
1-2 teaspoons of peanut butter
1/2 teaspoon of chocolate Slim Fast or any protein type powder
3 ice cubes (chopped)
Sweetener (optional)

Place milk or yogurt in a blender. Add other ingredients and blend at medium speed until it thickens. Pour into glass and garnish with sliced bananas.
Note: Use any combination of fruits.

This is great for an after school snack. Make ahead of time and have a welcome treat waiting in the freezer as a shake or in the refrigerator as a refreshing energy drink.

Iced Tea

Jo Ann M. Nuetzel, Immaculate Heart of Mary, Baynesville

5 cups boiling water
6 tea bags
2 limes (juice only)
3/4 cup sugar
32 ice cubes

Place tea bags in boiling water. Steep 5 minutes. Discard tea bags. Add juice and sugar. When sugar dissolves, add ice cubes. Refrigerate. Enjoy anytime. Note: Tastes great warmed up on a chilly day.

Back in the early 70's my neighbor always served delicious iced tea year round. I could never get my tea to taste the same when I made it. Then I found the above recipe (Discover Brunch Cookbook by Ruth MacPherson) and have been making it ever since.

"Orangey" Almond Punch

Susan Lichke, Baltimore

2 cups orange juice, frozen	1 tablespoon vanilla
2 cups water	1 tablespoon almond extract
2 cups sugar	2 quarts of Ginger Ale
3/4 cup lemon juice	1 orange

In a saucepan, boil together sugar and water until sugar is dissolved. Cool. In a large container combine orange juice, lemon juice, vanilla and almond extracts and add to cooled sugar syrup. (Reserve 1-1/2 cups for *Orangy Ice cubes.) Pour remaining punch into large punch bowl and add Ginger Ale. Before serving add orangey ice cubes.

*"Orangey" Ice Cubes

Slice orange, (do not peel) into 12 pieces and place pieces in ice cube tray. Pour reserve punch mixture into trays over orange pieces and freeze overnight.

Peppermint Cooler

America's Best Low-Fat Recipes

3/4 cup vanilla low-fat ice cream
3/4 cup skim milk
5 peppermint candies
Ice cubes

Blend first three ingredients in blender until smooth. Add ice cubes to bring mixture to a two cup level. Blend until smooth. Makes 2 cups.

Pineapple Pleasure

America's Best Low-Fat Recipes
Aileen Sohn, Baltimore

1 (6 ounce can) frozen lemonade concentrate
1-1/2 cups ice cubes
1 pint pineapple sherbet
1 (10 ounce can) ginger ale

Blend first three ingredients until smooth. Spoon into pitcher and stir in ginger ale.

Mock Sangria

Aileen Sohn, Baltimore

2 (25.3 ounce bottles) sparkling Catawba
1 (48 ounce bottle) cranberry-apple juice
2 (10 ounce bottles) club soda
1/4 cup lime juice
1-1/2 tablespoon instant tea

Combine all ingredients; chill. Serve with lemon and lime wedges. Makes 12 cups.

This recipe is a favorite from "America's Best Low-Fat Recipes"

Strawberry Cheesecake Shake

America's Best Low-Fat Recipes

Jeanette Sohn, Baltimore

1 (10 ounce package) frozen sliced strawberries in syrup, thawed
1/3 cup reduced-fat cream cheese, softened
1 pint vanilla low-fat ice cream
1/2 cup skim milk

Blend all ingredients in an electric blender or processor until smooth. Serve immediately in tall glasses, garnished with fresh strawberries.

Tropical Cooler

Say Yes to Less Cookbook

Jeanette Sohn, Baltimore

1 cup pineapple juice, chilled
2 tablespoons honey
1 cup orange sherbet
1 cup frozen vanilla yogurt

In blender, combine all ingredients. Cover and blend 30 to 60 seconds or until smooth. Serve immediately. Garnish with fresh orange slice or fresh strawberry.

Appetizers

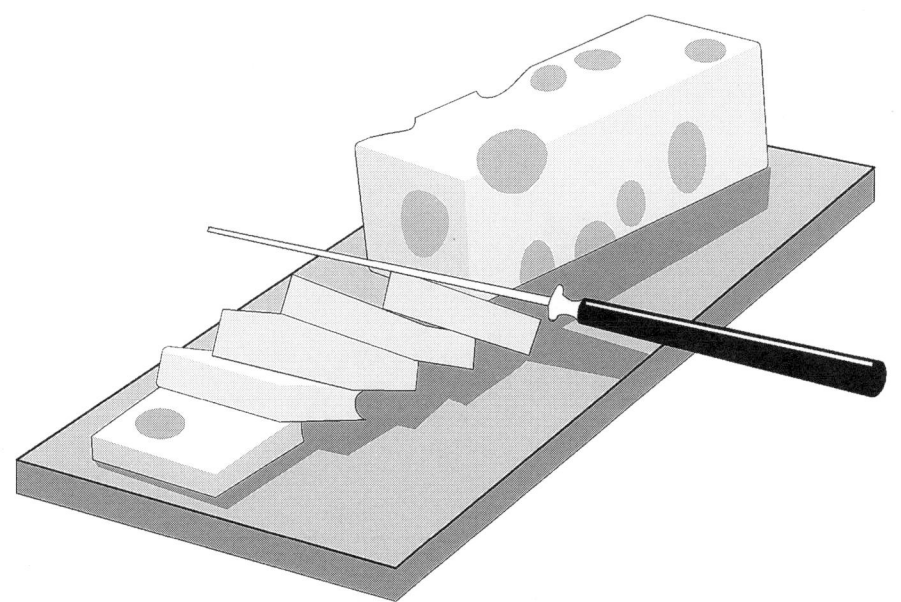

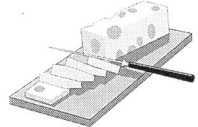

Asparagus Dip

Say Yes to Less Cookbook

Aileen Sohn, Baltimore

1/2 cup low-fat sour cream
1/3 cup low-fat mayonnaise
1/4 teaspoon garlic powder
Dash hot pepper sauce
1 (10-1/2 ounce can) asparagus spears, drained

Combine ingredients in small bowl and stir well. Cover and refrigerate overnight. Serve with crackers or small wedges of crusty rolls.

Light and Lively Cheese Ball

Eleanor Trimley, St. Joseph Parish

2 (8 ounce packages) light cream cheese, softened
1 tablespoon of caraway seeds
2 green onions, chopped (include greens)
1 tablespoon Worcestershire sauce
1-1/2 cup minced parsley
Chopped nuts

Blend all ingredients except the nuts. Form cheese mixture into balls or log shapes and roll in chopped nuts. Place on a small plate and garnish with parsley. Serve with crackers.

Dilled Chicken Bites

Cindy Wellenburg, Baltimore

1/3 cup olive oil
3 tablespoons reduced fat mayonnaise
2 tablespoons white wine vinegar
1/2 teaspoon salt
1/2 teaspoon pepper
2 cups chopped chicken
1/2 cucumber, finely chopped
1/4 cup onion, finely chopped
2 tablespoons dillweed, fresh, chopped
4 heads endive

Blend first five ingredients in medium bowl. Stir in chicken and next three ingredients. Set aside. Separate endive leaves and spoon 1 tablespoon of chicken mixture onto each leaf. Makes about 50 appetizers.

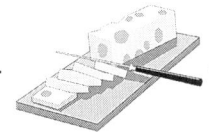

Chili Cheese Log

Elaine M. Carson, St. Edmond's Parish, Rehoboth Beach

1 pound Velveeta cheese
4 ounces cream cheese
1 tablespoon lemon juice
1/4 teaspoon garlic powder
Dash of red pepper
1 teaspoon instant minced onion (soaked)
1/4 cup finely chopped pecans
1 tablespoon chili powder
1 tablespoon paprika

Soften cheeses at room temperature and combine with lemon juice, garlic powder, red pepper and onion. Stir in nuts. Shape into rolls approximately 1-1/2 inches in diameter and 6 inches in length. Combine chili powder and paprika. Roll cheese logs in mixture. Wrap each log in plastic wrap and refrigerate. This recipe will make four logs.

Every Christmas Eve our neighbor in Bowie, Maryland made us Chili Cheese Logs beautifully packaged with several varieties of crackers. Before we retired and moved to the coastal region of Delaware, I asked our neighbor for the recipe so that I could continue to make this delicious recipe for our family and friends at Christmas.

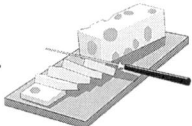

Hot Crab Dip

Marge Crossin, Holy Spirit Church, Joppatowne

1 (8 ounce package) cream cheese
1/2 cup of mayonnaise
1 (6 ounce can) backfin crab-meat
1/2 cup slivered almonds
2 tablespoons dry white wine
2 green onions, chopped
1 tablespoon dried parsley
1 tablespoon horseradish
1/4 teaspoon Worcestershire Sauce
1 tablespoon Old Bay Seasoning

Place cream cheese in medium glass mixing bowl. Microwave cream cheese for 2 minutes. Add mayonnaise, onion, parsley and mix thoroughly. The dip can be used in this form or you can now add the additional ingredients. If you choose to add the other ingredients stir in and then microwave for an additional 4-5 minutes or until hot. Note: This recipe may also be placed in the oven at 350 degrees for 20 minutes or until bubbly. Serve with crackers or cocktail rye bread.

Our family always enjoys this recipe throughout the year. It is great for parties and vanishes very quickly.

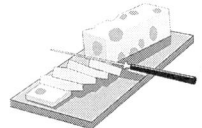

Grapes and Cheese

Jo Ann M. Nuetzel, Immaculate Heart of Mary, Baynesville

Bunch of green and purple seedless grapes
Swiss cheese, cubed

Wash grapes and set aside. Cut cheese in cube sizes. Alternate cheese and grapes on skewers or toothpicks. Arrange on plate or serving dish. Crackers or goldfish can be served on the side.

This recipe is simple and easy, but has always been a hit as a light appetizer served with wine or a nice sherry.

Jalapeno Peppers

America's Best Low-Fat Recipes

Jeanette Sohn, Baltimore

3/4 cup dry breadcrumbs
`1 tablespoon paprika
3 (12 ounce jars) whole pickled jalapeno peppers
1 (8 ounce package) reduced fat cream cheese, softened
1 (8-3/4 ounce can) whole kernel corn, drained
1 green onion
1/2 cup egg substitute

Combine breadcrumbs and paprika in small bowl. Set aside. Slit peppers down one side and carefully remove seeds and pulp. Combine cream cheese, corn, and green onions. Stuff each pepper with 1 tablespoon cheese mixture. Dip in egg substitute and roll in breadcrumbs mixture. Arrange on a baking sheet coated with cooking spray. Bake at 350 degrees for 10 minutes. Makes 40 appetizers.

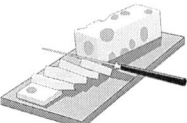

Oyster Crackers

Donna Schissler, St. Clare Church, Essex

1 package Hidden Valley Ranch Style dressing
1 tablespoon garlic
1 tablespoon lemon pepper
1 tablespoon dill weed, chopped
3/4 cup oil
1 (16 ounce box) oyster crackers

Mix all ingredients and pour over oyster crackers. Store in air tight container. May use as garnish on your salad, in your favorite soup, or just a tasty snack by itself.

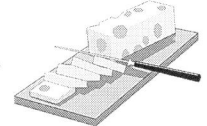

Grilled Oysters, Texas Style

Sue Rhinehardt, Our Lady of the Fields Church, Millersville

1/2 cup spicy barbecue sauce
1/4 cup Worcestershire sauce
2 tablespoons lemon juice
1 tablespoon olive oil
Salt and pepper to taste
4 garlic cloves, minced
4 dozen oysters in a shell, scrubbed
1/4 cup chopped fresh parsley
8 lemon wedges

Combine the first seven ingredients in a small saucepan and stir well. Prepare grill. Place saucepan containing barbecue sauce on grill rack. Place oysters on grill rack and grill 5 minutes or until a few oysters begin to open. Remove oysters from heat. Carefully open oysters with an oyster knife, leaving on half shell. Sprinkle oysters with parsley, and drizzle with barbecue sauce. Serve with lemon wedges.

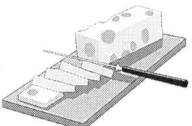

Spicy Party Mix

Jo Ann M. Nuetzel, Immaculate Heart of Mary, Baynesville

3 cups bite-sized shredded rice squares
3 cups bite-sized shredded wheat squares
3/4 cups peanuts (unsalted is optional)
3/4 cups pretzels, small size (unsalted is optional)
1/3 cup grated Parmesan cheese
1/3 cup cooking oil (light oil is optional)
1/2 teaspoon hot pepper sauce
1 teaspoon of chili powder
1/4 teaspoon of garlic powder
2 cups chow mein noodles

In large shallow baking pan combine cereals, peanuts, and pretzels. In a mixing bowl combine oil and pepper sauce and drizzle over cereal mixture until well coated. In a separate bowl combine Parmesan cheese, chili powder, and garlic powder. Stir into cereal mixture. Bake in a 300 degree oven for 20 minutes, stirring after 10 minutes. Stir in chow mein noodles. Bake an additional 10 minutes.

Several years ago my husband was advised to lower his sodium intake. This recipe provided a tasty alternative to salty snacks, and is delicious.

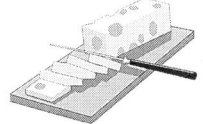

Taco Dip

Sue Rinehart, Baltimore

1 (16 ounce container) of low-fat sour cream
1 package taco mix
1 (8 ounce package) shredded cheddar cheese
Diced raw vegetables of your choice (lettuce, peppers,
    tomatoes, olives, onions, etc.)

Combine sour cream and taco mix. Place mixture on platter and layer your choice of raw vegetables on top. Sprinkle cheddar cheese over vegetables. Serve with nacho chips.

Include more chicken and fish in your menus. Choose beef, pork, and veal and select only lean cuts; trim all visible fat.

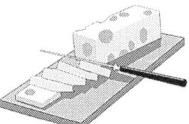

Cheese-Stuffed Zucchini

Kathleen Dotterwiech, Kingsville

3 small zucchinis
1/4 cup egg substitute, beaten
1/2 cup low-fat ricotta cheese
1/2 cup low-fat cheddar cheese
1/2 cup chopped fresh parsley
1/4 cup bread crumbs

Slice zucchini lengthwise into halves. Steam until just barely tender. Drain. Pat dry and scoop out pulp. Combine egg, cheeses and parsley. Fill zucchini shells. Sprinkle with bread crumbs. Arrange zucchini in baking dish greased with tub safflower margarine. Bake at 350 degrees for 25 minutes. Place under broiler 2-3 minutes to brown bread crumbs.

Soups & Salads

Barley and Lentil Soup

Phyllis Gloss, St. Ursula, Parkville

1/2 cup pearl barley
2 cups dried lentils
2 tablespoons olive oil
1 large onion, chopped
1 leek, washed, coarsely chopped
4 carrots, cut into 1 inch chunks
2 stalks of celery, cut diagonally
2 cloves garlic, chopped
1 teaspoon salt
1 teaspoon seasoned salt
1 teaspoon dried Italian herbs, crushed
2 bay leaves
Dash cayenne pepper

Rinse and drain barley and lentils. Heat oil in large pot. Add onion and garlic. Cook slowly, stirring frequently until vegetables are soft. Add leek, carrots and celery and continue cooking. Add seasonings, barley and lentils. Stir well. Add enough water to cover vegetables, about 3 quarts. Slowly bring to boil. Cover and simmer about 1 hour or until barley and lentils are tender. Add more water as necessary. Remove bay leaves before serving.

Beef Vegetable Soup

Gerry Staib, St. Joseph Parish, Fullerton

1 pound ground sirloin (lean)
1 large can V-8 juice
1 box mixed vegetables (frozen)
1/2 teaspoon onion powder (optional)
1 bay leaf
1 packet of Sweet and Low
 Parsley
 Water as needed

Brown ground sirloin in a non-stick pan on low heat. Drain well. Add V-8 juice to meat mixture and simmer for 15 minutes. Add vegetables, onion powder, bay leaf, sugar packet and parsley. Continue to simmer on a low heat until meat is tender.

Our Family's Midwestern Chowder

Joan Anne Rubis, St. Mary's Parish, Annapolis

1 (6-1/2 ounce can) water packed tuna
1 (12 ounce can) Mexicorn, drained
1 (10-1/4 ounce can) condensed cream of potato soup
1 cup grated American processed cheese, low fat
1 tablespoon instant chopped onion
1/4 teaspoon thyme
1 tablespoon Worcestershire Sauce
1/4 teaspoon freshly ground pepper
2 cups half and half (light or regular)
Crisp bacon, crumbled (optional)

In heavy 4 quart saucepan, combine all ingredients except bacon. Cook over medium heat, stirring occasionally until mixture starts to bubble and cheese is melted. (approximately 10-15 minutes) Top each serving with bacon if desired.

This is an exceptional "stick to your ribs" chowder. We enjoyed it on Ash Wednesday or Good Friday when meat was not an option. Our Judy, especially enjoyed this chowder and now prepares it for her own family.

She-Crab Soup

Patricia V. Saunders, St. Ursula Parish, Parkville

1 tablespoon margarine
1 teaspoon flour
1 quart skim milk
2 cups white crab-meat and crab eggs
1/8 teaspoon mace
1/2 teaspoon salt (optional)
1/8 teaspoon pepper
4 tablespoons sherry
1/4 pint whipping cream (optional)

Melt margarine in the top of a double boiler or microwave until melted. Add flour. Add the milk gradually, stirring constantly. Add crabmeat and eggs and all seasonings except sherry. Cook slowly for about 20 minutes. To serve, add 1 tablespoon of warmed sherry to individual bowls and pour soup mixture over sherry. Top with whipping cream if desired. Sprinkle with parsley.

Lemon Waldorf Salad

Jo Ann M. Nuetzel, Immaculate Heart of Mary, Baynesville

1/2 cup Hellman's mayonnaise (may use low fat)
1 tablespoon sugar
1 tablespoon milk
1 teaspoon grated lemon rind
3 apples, cored and diced
1 cup sliced celery
1/2 cup chopped walnuts (may substitute raisins)
2 tablespoons lemon juice

Stir together mayonnaise, sugar, milk and lemon rind. Cover and chill. Toss together rest of ingredients. Cover and chill. Before serving, toss dressing with apple mixture. Serve on lettuce pieces and garnish with cherry, strawberry or pineapple chunks.

This recipe has been around since 1979 when I cut it out of a Better Homes and Gardens magazine. It's Yummy!

Lenten Lentil Soup

Alice (Murphe) Tuder, Church of the Crucifixion, Glen Burnie

1 (16 ounce bag) lentils, sorted and washed
1 cup chopped carrot
1 cup chopped onion
1 cup chopped celery
1 (28 ounce can) tomato puree
1 (15 ounce can) of whole tomatoes
1 (10 ounce package) frozen spinach
1/2 cup uncooked macaroni (optional)
2 teaspoons minced garlic
1/2 teaspoon salt

Fresh ground pepper
1 teaspoon of Mrs. Dash
   Seasoning
8-10 cups of water
2 bay leaves

Combine all ingredients except macaroni. Bring to boil and reduce heat. Simmer for approximately 20 minutes, stirring occasionally. Add macaroni and cook 15 minutes or until macaroni and lentils are completely cooked. Keeps well in refrigerator. Serves about 20 people.

Several years ago as a result of "Renew" three other ladies and myself formed a group called "Prayer Network". As one of our ideas to promote prayer in our church, we decided to offer Lenten Suppers before Stations of the Cross during Lent. I don't mind telling you how scared we were. There was no way to know how many people would show up. Stations went from 6 to 8 people to well over 60. We couldn't believe it, and there was never a time that we ran out of food. We felt Jesus was there with us on those Fridays and, like the miracle of the loaves and fishes, there was always plenty to go around.

Sunshine Orange Salad

Patti Medinger, Church of Nativity, Timonium

6 cups of fresh lettuce (may use romaine or spinach)
1 cup sliced fresh mushrooms
4 green onions (chopped)
1/4 cup bacon bits (optional)
2 teaspoons cornstarch
1/2 teaspoon of grated orange rind
1 cup of orange juice
2 oranges, sliced in half and peeled
Fresh ground pepper
1/2 cup sliced green pepper
1/2 cup sliced red pepper
1 small can mandarin oranges

In a large decorative glass bowl, combine lettuce, mushrooms, and onions. set aside. In a skillet add orange peel, orange juice, cornstarch and fresh pepper. Cook and stir until mixture thickens. remove from heat. Pour liquid mixture over lettuce and garnish with peppers, sliced oranges, bacon bits, and mandarin oranges.

Romaine and Walnut Toss

Aileen Sohn, Baltimore

1/4 cup honey
1/4 cup oil
1 tablespoon vinegar
1/4 teaspoon dry mustard
4 cups Romaine lettuce
1/4 cup walnuts, chopped

In small bowl, combine honey, oil, vinegar, and mustard and blend well. Cover and refrigerate until ready to serve. In medium bowl, combine lettuce and walnuts. To serve drizzle dressing over salad. Makes four servings. A perfect anytime salad.

Seashell Shrimp Salad

Pat Richardson, St. Ursula, Parkville

1 (6 ounce package) medium shell noodles
1/2 pound frozen shrimp, cooked
1/2 cup celery, chopped
1/4 cup green pepper, chopped
1 (8 ounce carton) low-fat lemon yogurt
Salt and pepper to taste
Lettuce leaves

Cook noodles as directed, drain and rinse. In large bowl combine cooked noodles, and remaining ingredients. Cover and refrigerate to blend flavors.

Thin Man's "Stone Soup"

Joan Anne Rubis, St. Mary's Parish, Annapolis

1 clean stone from the garden
2 stalks of celery, diced
3-4 carrots, chopped
1 large onion
1/2 head of cabbage, chopped
46 ounces of tomato juice
2 cups water
6 beef, chicken or vegetable bouillon cubes

Combine all of the above ingredients and simmer for one hour. In place of bouillon cubes you may use one packet of beef stew season mix. Before serving, remove your "Soup Stone."

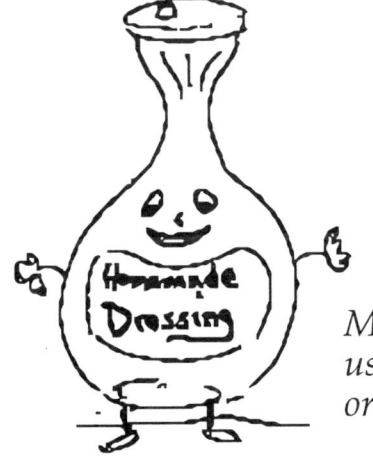

Make your own dressings by using low-fat yogurt, buttermilk, or flavored vinegar.

Notes

Breads

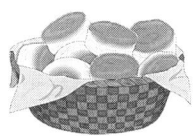

Healthy Banana Muffins

Patti Medinger, Church of Nativity, Timonium

1 cup flour
1/2 cup whole wheat flour
1/4 cup sugar
2-1/2 teaspoons baking powder
1/4 teaspoon baking soda
1-1/2 teaspoons cinnamon
1/4 teaspoon salt
1/4 cup wheat germ
1/4 cup sunflower seeds (may substitute chopped nuts)
1/3 cup skim milk
1/3 cup light oil
1/4 cup honey
1 egg
2 medium bananas, mashed

In a large bowl, mix flours, sugar, baking powder, baking soda, cinnamon, and salt. Stir in wheat germ, sunflower seeds or nuts. Set aside. Mix the milk, egg, oil, honey, and banana. Add the wet mixture to the dry mixture and stir until moistened. Spoon batter into muffin pans, filling each cup about two-thirds full. Bake for 15-20 in a 400 degree preheated oven. Remove from oven and from tin. Serve in air tight bag after completely cooled.

Cinnamon Muffins

Diane Thompson Griggs, Phoenix

2 cups unsifted all purpose flour
1/4 cup instant non-fat dried milk
3 tablespoons sugar
3 teaspoons baking powder
Salt
2 egg whites
1 cup water
1/4 cup light cooking oil
1/2 teaspoon cinnamon

Stir flour, instant milk, 2 tablespoon of sugar, baking powder, and salt in medium bowl. Set aside. Beat eggs in small bowl. Add water and oil to egg mixture. Add egg mixture to flour mixture and stir until blended. (mixture will be lumpy) Spoon into a 12 cup greased muffin tin. Sprinkle remaining sugar over the top of the mixture. Bake for 25 minutes in a 400 degree oven. Remove from oven and remove from cups. Serve warm.

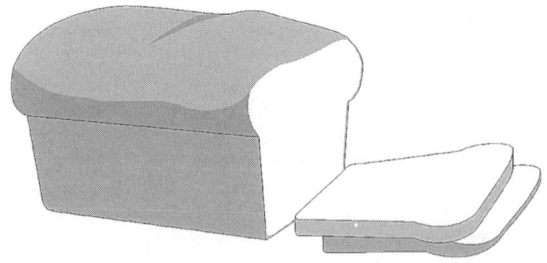

Garlic Knots

Tina Lewis, Timonium

1 (11-ounce can) Pillsbury Soft Breadsticks
2 tablespoons oil
2 garlic cloves, minced (may use garlic powder)

Heat oven to 350 degrees. Unroll dough and separate at perforation to form 8 strips. Shape each strip into a knot and place on ungreased cookie sheet about 2 inches apart. In a small bowl combine oil and garlic. Brush each knot with garlic mixture. Bake at 350 degrees for 15 minutes. Serve warm.

Skillet Garlic Toast

Tina Lewis, Timonium

6 tablespoons margarine
1/2 teaspoon garlic powder
6 slices French bread, cut 3/4 inch thick
2 tablespoons grated Parmesan cheese

In a small bowl, combine margarine and garlic powder and mix well. Spread evenly on both sides of bread slices. Heat skillet over medium- high heat until hot. Place bread in skillet and toast 1-2 minutes until golden brown. Remove from pan and sprinkle with Parmesan cheese.

Mint Julep Bread

Marge Crossin, Joppatowne

2 cups flour
3-1/2 teaspoons baking powder
1/2 teaspoon salt
2-3 teaspoons butter
2 tablespoons sugar
1/2 cup milk
2 eggs
1/3 cup plump raisins
(marinated in 1 teaspoon of bourbon or brandy)

In a medium size bowl, combine flour, baking powder and salt. With a pastry blender work in the butter. Add the sugar. Mix well. Add milk gradually. Add eggs. Beat vigorously with a wooden spoon or rotary beater. Fold in marinated raisins. Bake in greased and lightly floured loaf pan for 30 minutes in a 350 degree oven. Do not overbake. Cool. Spread frosting.

Mint Julep Frosting

Marge Crossin, Joppatowne

1 cup sifted confectioners sugar
1/3 cup melted mint jelly

Blend together until smooth. Add additional sugar for thicker consistency. Spread over cooled bread.

This is a great bread to serve on St. Patrick's Day!

My Sister Josephine's Cheap Russian Bread

Theresa M. Hallow, St. Mary's Parish, Annapolis

8 cups flour
3 tablespoons sugar
1 tablespoon salt
2 cups lukewarm water

1/4 cup Crisco shortening
1 package dry yeast
1/2 cup lukewarm water
1/3 cup Crisco oil

Mix flour salt and solid shortening. Set aside. Combine sugar, yeast and 1/2 cup water in small mixing bowl and wait until mixture "foams". Add "foaming mixture" to flour mixture. Add 2 cups water and knead dough until it makes a ball. Add liquid oil and continue kneading until you have a nice elastic ball of dough. Cover with greased wax paper, tea towel and wrap entire bowl in large towel or blanket (keep dough out of drafts). Pound down in 90 minutes. Let rise another 90 minutes. Punch down, then form into 3 small loaves or 2 large loaves. grease bread pans well before placing dough in them. Let rise until double, at least 60 minutes. Bake in preheated 350 degree oven for 60 minutes. Remove from oven and lightly butter top of bread. Let cool before slicing.

This recipe is dedicated to my sister, Josephine Mihalko from Sacred Heart Parish in Portage, Pennsylvania. At Easter time she would make the loaves round and place a cross on top made from dough. One of her special loaves was placed in a linen covered basket, also containing colored Easter eggs, a small ham, homemade beet horseradish, kielbasi and candy. It was blessed by the Parish Priest and then after Easter Vigil we could taste the "Blessed Food". My sister taught me patiently how to make this special bread for my own family.

Toasted Rye Loaf

Tina Lewis, Timonium

1/3 cup margarine
1 tablespoon horseradish
1 tablespoon prepared mustard
1 garlic clove, minced or 1/2 teaspoon garlic powder
1 pound round rye

Heat oven to 350 degrees. In a small bowl, combine all ingredients except bread and mix well. Slice loaf into 1/2 inch slices, cutting to, but not through bottom of loaf. Spread one side of each slice with margarine mixture. Wrap loaf in foil. Bake at 350 degrees for 30 to 35 minutes or until thoroughly heated.

Three Seeds Bread

Martha Calabrese, Church of the Resurrection, Ellicott City

3 eggs, beaten
1/2 cup oil
1/2 cup milk
1 cup sugar
2-1/2 cup flour
1 tablespoon baking powder
1 tablespoon baking soda
1/2 teaspoon salt
1 tablespoon cinnamon
1/2 cup maraschino cherries
1-1/3 cups coconut
1/2 cup raisins
2 cup shredded carrots

Beat together eggs, milk, oil and sugar. Set aside. Sift together flour, baking powder, baking soda, cinnamon, salt. Add dry mixture to egg mixture. Stir until moist. Add all remaining ingredients. Pour into two 8x4 inch loaf pans that have been greased or sprayed with a cooking oil. Bake 45 minutes in a 350 degree oven. (If you use a larger loaf pan, bake 1 hour). Cool in pan 10 minutes. Store in refrigerator. Serve with whipped butter or whipped cream cheese.

Main Dishes

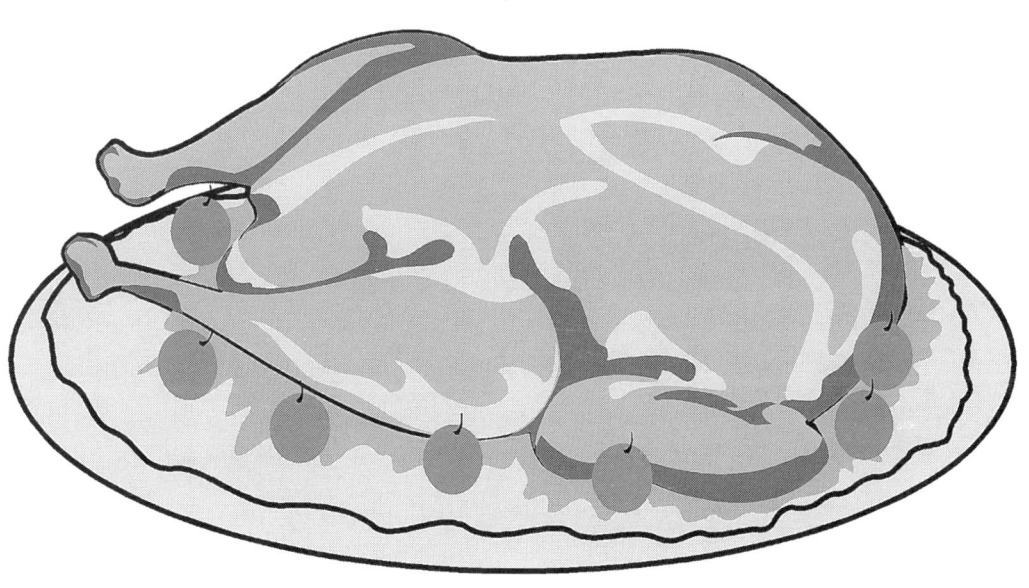

Zesty Beans and Rice

Pat Kenny, St. Philip Neri Parish, Linthicum Heights

1 (16 ounce can) pork and beans in a tomato sauce
1 cup frozen whole kernel corn
1 cup of prepared rice
1 medium onion, chopped
1 tablespoon packed brown sugar
3 tablespoons barbecue sauce
1/8 teaspoon pepper
1/2 cup water

In a 2 quart saucepan combine chopped onion and water and heat over low heat until onion is soft. Add the beans, corn, rice, brown sugar, barbecue sauce and pepper. Cook over low heat until heated through. Stir occasionally to avoid sticking. Yields 4 servings

Beef Pepper and Mushroom Stir-Fry

Pat Blakely, Church of Nativity, Timonium

1 teaspoon olive oil, divided
6 ounces beef tenderloin
1/2 cup sliced shallots
1/2 cup green pepper, sliced into 1/4 inch strips
1/2 cup red peppers, sliced into 1/4 inch strips
2 cups mushroom caps
1/4 cup dry white wine
1/2 cup no-salt beef broth
1/2 teaspoon chopped fresh basil
1/4 teaspoon salt
1/4 teaspoon pepper
1-1/2 cups hot cooked rice

Heat 1/2 teaspoon of olive oil in large non-stick pan. Add beef and stir fry for 2 minutes. Remove beef and set aside. In clean skillet heat remaining 1/2 teaspoon olive oil. Then add pepper strips, mushroom caps, garlic and stir fry 1 minute. Add broth and simmer 1 minute. Add wine and heat an additional minute. Add beef to mixture and continue to stir-fry on low heat. Add basil, salt, pepper. Serve with hot rice.

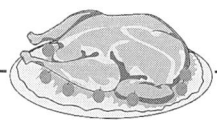

Stuffed Beef Tenderloins

Nancy Reitz, Pastoral Associate for Religious Education, SS. Philip and James Church, Baltimore

    Vegetable cooking spray
    1 pound fresh mushrooms, sliced
    1 cup chopped green onions
    1/4 cup chopped fresh parsley
    1 (5-6 pound) beef tenderloin
    1/2 teaspoon of seasoning, herb blend
    1/2 cup of soy sauce, reduced sodium
    1/3 cup dry sherry
    3 tablespoons honey
    2 tablespoons brown sugar
    1 tablespoon vegetable oil
    2 cloves garlic, minced

Coat a large, nonstick skillet with cooking spray and place over medium heat. Add mushrooms and green onions. Sauté until tender. Drain. Stir in parsley. Set aside. Trim excess fat from tenderloin. Cut tenderloin lengthwise from top to within 1/2 inch of bottom, leaving bottom connected. Sprinkle with herb seasoning. Spoon mushroom mixture into opening of tenderloin and pull sides together. Tie tenderloin securely with string. Place in large, shallow dish and set aside. Combine soy sauce and remaining ingredients and pour over tenderloin. Cover and refrigerate at least 8 hours, basting occasionally. Drain tenderloin and place on a rack in a roasting pan. Bake at 425 degrees for 45 to 60 minutes. Transfer to serving platter and let stand 15 minutes.

Quick and Easy Beef and Beans

Carole Ewing, Baltimore

2 pounds lean ground beef
2 (8 ounce cans) tomato sauce
1 green pepper, diced
1 red pepper, diced
2 (8 ounce cans) diced tomatoes
1 pkg frozen green beans, thawed

Cook ground beef and drain. In Dutch oven combine ground beef and remaining ingredients. Simmer on low heat until green beans are tender. Serve with rice, potatoes or pasta.

JoAnn's Beef Tips Over Noodles

JoAnn Dannenfelser, St. Francis de Sales and St Elizabeth

1-1/2 pounds beef tips
4 green peppers, quartered
3 large onions, quartered
1/4 cup beef broth

2 cups water
1 pound whole mushrooms
1 can whole tomatoes
1 (16 ounce package) wide egg noodles

Brown beef tips. Sauté onions, green peppers, and mushrooms in butter. Add water and beef broth to beef tips and simmer 10 minutes. Add onions, green peppers, mushrooms, and tomatoes to beef. Let pot simmer for 20 minutes. Arrange beef tips and vegetables over noodles and serve.

Broccoli and Chicken Over Pasta

Lisa Goodwin, Baltimore

1/2 pound boneless chicken breast, cubed
2 bottles fat-free Italian dressing
2 cups broccoli, cut in small pieces
2 cups mushrooms, sliced
1 red pepper, cut in strips
1 (8 ounce package) pasta

Marinate chicken in Italian dressing overnight. Slowly cook marinated chicken pieces in a non-stick frying pan until chicken is completely cooked. Add more Italian dressing as needed to prevent sticking. Add the broccoli and pepper and cook an additional 5 minutes. Add the mushrooms and cook another 10 minutes. (Cooking time will vary according to how crispy you like your vegetables.) Serve chicken/vegetables over hot pasta.

Roast meat on a rack to allow fat to drip off, then discard fat.

Broccoli Lasagna

Diane Thompson-Griggs, Phoenix

1 large bunch broccoli
3/4 teaspoon salt (optional)
1 (16 ounce carton) low-fat cottage cheese
2 egg whites
1/4 cup grated parmesan cheese
3 tablespoons flour
1/2 teaspoon Italian herb seasoning
1 (15 ounce jar) spaghetti sauce
1 (8 ounce package) mozzarella cheese (shredded)
Vegetable cooking spray

In 10 inch skillet over medium heat 2 cups water and salt if desired. Slice broccoli lengthwise into 1/4 inch thick slices. Bring water and broccoli to boil. Reduce heat to low and cover and simmer 5 minutes. Drain. Preheat oven to 375 degrees. In food processor, blend cottage cheese, egg whites, parmesan cheese, flour and Italian herb seasonings until smooth. Spray 12 X 8 inch baking dish with vegetable cooking spray. In baking dish arrange half of broccoli in single layer, top with cottage cheese mixture. Continue layering with remaining ingredients. Spoon spaghetti sauce over broccoli and sprinkle with mozzarella cheese. Bake uncovered 35 minutes or until hot and bubbly in center. Let stand 5 minutes for easier serving. Use pancake turner for serving. Makes 6 servings.

This is a super easy and delicious low-fat lasagna.

Cabbage with Cheese

Kathy Olson, Ellicott City

5 cups shredded cabbage
2 cups cooked rice
1/8 teaspoon black pepper
1/3 cup milk
1 (10-1/2 ounce can) condensed cream of mushroom soup
1 cup grated sharp cheddar cheese

Cook the cabbage in a small amount of boiling salted water until just tender, about 10 minutes. Place the rice in a greased 1-1/2 quart oven dish. Top with cabbage. Sprinkle with the black pepper. Mix together the milk and mushroom soup. Pour over the cabbage. Cover with the cheese. Place in a preheated 350 degree oven. Bake about 40 minutes or until cheese begins to brown. Serve immediately.

Cabbage Supreme

Phyllis Gloss, St. Ursula Parish, Parkville

8 ounce ground beef, cooked and drained
1/2 cup cabbage
8-10 ounce tomato juice
1 can green beans, French style
1/2 teaspoon oregano
1/2 teaspoon basil
1/2 teaspoon garlic
Dash red pepper flakes
Parmesan cheese

Combine all ingredients in large frying pan and cook for about 30 minutes or until cabbage is tender. Sprinkle Parmesan cheese on each serving.

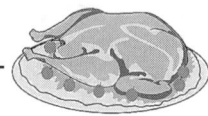

Curried Chicken

Doris Dannenfelser, St. Margaret Parish, Bel Air

1 large apple, unpeeled and chopped
1/4 cup sliced green onions
1 tablespoon curry powder
1 tablespoon water
1/2 (10-3/4 ounce) can cream of mushroom soup (undiluted)
1 cup skim milk
2 tablespoon minced fresh parsley
2 cups chopped, cooked chicken
1/2 cup plain, unsweetened low-fat yogurt
Quick cooking brown rice

Combine apple, green onions, curry powder and water in a medium saucepan. Cover and cook over medium heat until onions are tender. Add soup, milk and parsley, stirring until well blended. Add chicken and simmer 10 minutes. Reduce heat to low and stir in yogurt. Cook, stirring gently, until thoroughly heated. Serve over cooked rice.

Chicken Delicious

Gerry Staib, St. Joseph Parish, Fullerton

1-1/4 pounds chicken parts, skin removed
1/2 cup reduced-calorie sweet and spicy French dressing
2 tablespoons minced onion flakes
2 packets instant beef flavored broth mix

Preheat oven to 350 degrees. Place chicken in a shallow baking pan, that has been sprayed with a non-stick cooking spray. Combine remaining ingredients in a small bowl. Mix well and spread over chicken. Cover and bake 30 minutes. Remove cover, baste chicken and bake an additional 30 minutes. Makes four servings.

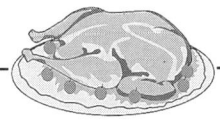

Chicken Dijon

Patti Medinger, Church of Nativity, Timonium

1-1/4 pounds, boneless,
  skinless chicken parts
1/2 teaspoon salt
1/4 teaspoon pepper
2 tablespoons plus 2 teaspoons
  margarine, melted

1/8 teaspoon garlic powder
2 teaspoons dried parsley flakes
1/2 teaspoon dried rosemary, crumbled
1/2 teaspoon paprika
1/4 teaspoon dried thyme
1 tablespoon plus 2 teaspoon Dijon mustard

Preheat oven to 350 degrees. Place chicken in a shallow baking dish that has been sprayed with a non-stick cooking spray. combine all remaining ingredients in a small bowl. Mix well and spread over chicken. Cover and bake 30 minutes. Remove cover and bake an additional 30 minutes.

Hawaiian Chicken Salad

Marge Crossin, Holy Spirit Parish, Joppatowne

2 quarts cut, cooked chicken breasts
2 cups celery, sliced
1 (5 ounce can) water chestnuts, sliced
1 pound seedless grapes
2-3 cups toasted, slivered almonds
3 cup mayonnaise

1 tablespoon curry powder
1 tablespoon soy sauce
1 teaspoon lemon juice
Pineapple chunks
Paprika

Combine cubed chicken, celery, water chestnuts, grapes and most of the almonds. (Reserve a few of the almonds for garnish) Mix mayonnaise with curry and soy sauce and a little lemon juice. Mix mayonnaise mixture with chicken-fruit mixture and chill several hours or overnight. When ready to serve, garnish with paprika, reserved almonds and drained pineapple chunks. Serves 18.

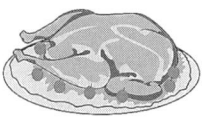

Be-Good-To-Mommy-Day...Honey Chicken

Joan Anne Rubis, St. Mary's Parish, Annapolis

6 skinless, boneless chicken breasts
1 egg (or 2 egg whites), slightly beaten
Seasoned bread crumbs
1 cup melted butter
4 tablespoons melted margarine
4 tablespoons honey
4 tablespoons white wine

Dip chicken breasts in beaten egg mixture and then into seasoned crumbs. Arrange chicken into lightly greased casserole dish. Combine other ingredients and pour over chicken. Cover and bake 35 minutes in a 350 degree oven. Remove cover and bake an additional 5 minutes. Serve with salad, baked potatoes and hot rolls.

Remove skin from chicken, which allows the meat to absorb seasonings and eliminates fat and unneeded calories.

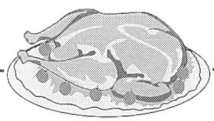

Mandarin Chicken and Rice

Jo Ann M. Nuetzel, Immaculate Heart of Mary Church, Baynesville

4 skinless, boneless chicken breasts
1 medium onion, chopped
3/4 teaspoon poultry seasoning
1 teaspoon olive oil
1 cup raw regular rice
1 cup reduced salt chicken broth
1/2 cup water
Grated orange peel
2 cans drained mandarin oranges
2 tablespoons sliced almonds

Spray large non-stick skillet with non-stick cooking spray. Pat chicken breasts dry with paper toweling. Over medium heat, lightly brown chicken on one side (2 to 3 minutes). Remove chicken. In same skillet, over medium heat sauté onion with poultry seasoning in olive oil. Add rice, chicken broth, water, and orange peel. Bring to boil. Reduce heat. Arrange chicken, brown side up on rice. Cover and cook over low heat for 20 minutes or until chicken is tender. Remove chicken. Add orange segments and almonds and heat briefly. Arrange rice mixture and chicken on serving platter. Sprinkle with chopped parsley.

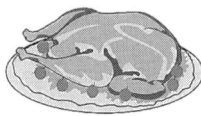

Orange-Herb Chicken

Kathy Olson, St. Paul Church, Ellicott City

2-1/2 to 3 pounds skinless, boneless chicken breast
1 cup orange juice
1/4 cup vegetable oil
1/4 cup orange marmalade
2 teaspoons grated orange rind
1 teaspoon dried whole basil
1 teaspoon dried whole oregano
1/2 teaspoon salt
1/2 teaspoon dried whole thyme
1/4 teaspoon pepper

Place chicken in a 13x9x2 inch baking dish. Combine orange juice and remaining ingredients in a small saucepan. Cook over medium heat 5 minutes or until marmalade melts. Stir occasionally. Pour orange juice mixture over chicken. Cover and refrigerate overnight. Remove chicken from marinade, reserving marinade. Place marinade in a small saucepan. Bring to a boil; reduce heat and simmer 5 minutes. Cover and bake chicken at 350 degrees for 30 minutes. Uncover and bake an additional 30 to 35 minutes or until tender. Makes 4 servings.

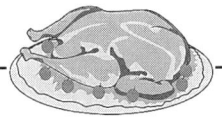

Easy Potato and Chicken Bake

Joan Anne Rubis, St. Mary's Church, Annapolis

1 pound potatoes, cut into medium-sized wedges
2-1/2 pounds chicken breast with bone
1/2 cup low-fat Italian dressing
1 tablespoon Italian seasonings
1/2 cup grated low-fat Parmesan cheese

Arrange chicken and potatoes into a 9x13 inch baking dish. Pour low-fat salad dressing over potatoes and chicken. Sprinkle with Italian seasonings and Parmesan cheese over entire top. Bake at 375 degrees for 1 hour or until chicken is completely cooked.

This is a perfect "thinking of you dish" for a friend or neighbor who may be under-the-weather.

Before making gravy, refrigerate meat drippings so that the chilled hardened fat can be lifted off the top and discarded.

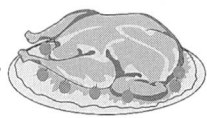

Easy To Please Chicken Reuben Bake

Joan Anne Rubis, St Mary's Church, Annapolis

6-8 skinless, boneless breasts of chicken
2 cups sauerkraut, drained
Fresh peppercorns, ground

1-1/4 cups low-calorie Russian dressing
3 slices Swiss cheese, low fat
Fresh parsley, chopped

Arrange chicken in lightly greased baking dish. Grind fresh pepper over chicken and layer with sauerkraut. Pour dressing evenly over everything and top with cheese. Cover and bake for 40-45 minutes at 325 degrees. Serve with boiled potatoes and hot crusty bread.

Chicken Scrapple

Clarine L. Ruszin, Patronage of the Mother of God, Baltimore

1/4 cup minced onion
1/2 teaspoon thyme
1/2 teaspoon poultry seasonings
2 tablespoon butter
1-3/4 cup chicken broth

1-3/4 cups chicken broth (second portion)
1 cup cornmeal
1/2 teaspoon salt
Pepper to taste
2 cups minced chicken

In a heavy saucepan sauté minced onion, thyme, poultry seasonings and butter until onion is softened. Stir in chicken broth. Bring to boil and then reduce heat to medium. In a bowl, combine second portion of chicken broth, cornmeal, salt and pepper. Add to onion mixture and cook for 20 minutes. Add chicken and mix thoroughly. Transfer to a loaf pan. Chill, covered with plastic wrap for at least 12 hours. Cut scrapple into slices, sprinkle with flour and brown in a frying pan.

Chrusciki or Bow Ties

Lorraine M. Whitely, St. Stephen's Parish, Bradshaw

6 egg yolks
6 tablespoons sugar
1 cup sweet cream
2 tablespoons rum or brandy
2 cups flour

Cream sugar and yolks until light and foamy. Add cream and rum. Add enough flour to divide into 2 or 3 parts. Roll one part of soft dough very thin on a floured surface. Cut into 1 inch strips and 5 to 6 inch length. Cut a small lengthwise strip in middle of each 6 inch strip and pull one end of strip through slit making a bow tie effect. Deep fry in heated vegetable oil until light golden brown. Drain on paper towels and sprinkle with confectioner's sugar.

No Polish wedding would be complete without these scrumptious favors. I can still picture my mother making this favorite delicate cookie, while we patiently waited our turn to sprinkle the sugar and savor the taste of love at its best!

Crab Crastini

Juliett Welsh, Baltimore

1/2 pound lump crabmeat
1/2 cup diced red pepper
2 tablespoons + 2 teaspoons reduced calorie mayonnaise
2 tablespoons parsley, chopped
1 tablespoon chives, chopped
1 tablespoon lime juice
1 tablespoon Dijon mustard
2 teaspoons Parmesan cheese
4-5 drops hot pepper sauce
1 (4 ounce loaf) Italian bread, cut into 16 slices

Preheat broiler and line broiler pan with foil. In medium bowl combine crabmeat, red pepper, mayonnaise, parsley, chives, lime juice, mustard, cheese and hot pepper sauce. Blend well. Spread 1 tablespoon of the crab mixture on each slice of bread. Place on broiler pan and broil 5-6 minutes or until lightly brown.

Maryland Crab Cakes "A La Catherine"

Diane Thompson Griggs, Phoenix

1 tablespoon non-fat mayonnaise
1 egg
Salt and pepper
1 tablespoon mustard
1-1/2 slices bread, crumbled
1 pound lump crab

Mix mayonnaise, mustard, egg, bread, salt and pepper in bowl. Add crab meat. Make into patties and sauté on low heat until crab cakes are brown on both sides.

Make Ahead Eggs Benedict

Barbara Hand, St. Ursula Parish, Parkville

4 English muffins
16 slices thin Canadian bacon
8 eggs
1/4 cup margarine
1/4 cup flour
1/8 teaspoon pepper
1 teaspoon paprika
1/8 teaspoon ground nutmeg
2 cups milk
2 cups shredded Swiss cheese
1/2 cup dry white wine
1/2 cup crushed corn flakes (about 1 cup before crushing)
1 tablespoon margarine, melted

In 13x9 inch pan arrange muffins and place 2 slices of bacon on each muffin half. Poach eggs and put one on each muffin. Set aside. For the sauce: melt margarine, stir in flour, paprika, nutmeg and pepper. Add milk. Cook until thick and bubbly. Stir in cheese until melted. Add wine. Carefully spoon over the muffins. Combine crushed flakes and 1 tablespoon margarine and sprinkle over muffins. Cover and chill overnight. Bake uncovered at 375 degrees for 20-25 minutes.

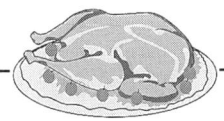

Egg Noodles with Poppy Seeds, Yogurt and Mushrooms

Patricia Richardson, St. Ursula Parish, Parkville

1 (8 ounce bag) medium egg noodles
1/4 cup sour cream
1/2 cup low-fat yogurt
1 tablespoon poppy seeds
1/8 teaspoon cayenne pepper
2 tablespoons virgin olive oil
1/2 pound mushrooms, thinly sliced
1 onion
1/4 teaspoon salt
1/2 cup dry white wine

In a small bowl, combine sour cream, yogurt, poppy seeds, cayenne pepper and 1 tablespoon oil. Set aside. In a large pot, cook egg noodles in 3 quarts of boiling water until tender or about 9 minutes. While the noodles are cooking, heat the remaining tablespoon of oil in a large, heavy-bottomed skillet over medium-high heat. Add the mushrooms and onion. Sprinkle with 1/4 teaspoon salt and cook stirring frequently until browned thoroughly. Add the wine to the skillet and continue cooking. Stir until almost all of the liquid has been absorbed, about 3 minutes. When the noodles are done, drain and add to skillet. Add the yogurt and poppy-seed mixture. Toss well and serve.

Fettuccine Pasquale

Father Paschal A. Morlino, OSB, Pastor, St. Benedict Parish, Baltimore

2 pounds fettuccine
1 pint half and half
8 eggs

1/2 cup chopped fresh parsley
1 stick margarine
1/4 cup Romano cheese, grated

Cook pasta al dente. While pasta is cooking, blend eggs, cream, and parsley. Drain pasta and pour back into pan on top of quartered margarine. Pour in mix and stir with vigor. Mix thoroughly. Hot pasta will cook eggs. Add cheese. Serve in soup plates. Top with fresh ground black pepper.

Note: Heat plates before serving.

Un-Fried French Fries

Pamela Gloss, Severna Park

5 large baking potatoes
2 large egg whites

1 tablespoon Cajun spice
Light vegetable oil cooking spray

Preheat oven to 400 degrees. Slice potatoes lengthwise into 1/4 inch ovals. Slice each oval lengthwise into match sticks. Coat a baking sheet with 3 sprays of vegetable oil. Combine the egg whites and Cajun spice in bowl. Add potatoes and mix well to coat completely. Pour coated potatoes on to baking sheet and spread evenly in a single layer. Bake for 40-45 minutes until fries are crispy. Turn every 6-8 minutes with spatula so they brown evenly.

This recipe is from Oprah Winfrey's cook, Rosie!

Oriental Meatballs

Diane Gardner, Baltimore

3/4 pound ground turkey
1 egg
1 small onion, grated
1 teaspoon dry mustard
Salt and pepper to taste

Pinch of Italian Seasoning
1/2 cup tomato juice
1/4 cup soy sauce
1 packet Sweet N' Low

Mix first six ingredients together and form into small meatballs. Pour sautéd ingredients into sauce pan. Add meatballs. Cover pan and simmer 1/2 hour.

Italian Meatballs

Mary Lou Harper, Church of Nativity, Timonium

3 slices white bread
1/2 cup milk
2 pounds ground meat (beef,
  pork, veal, Italian sausage or turkey)
2 (8 ounce cans) tomato sauce
2 eggs, slightly beaten

1/2 cup onion, chopped
1/8 teaspoon of salt
1/2 teaspoon pepper
2 teaspoons dried parsley
1 cup shredded mozzarella cheese
Grated parmesan cheese

Put bread slices on a plate. Pour milk over bread. Gently tear bread into tiny pieces and put into a large bowl. Add ground meat, *tomato sauce, eggs, onion, salt, pepper and parsley. Mix thoroughly until well blended. Take out of bowl and flatten mixture to form a rectangle approximately 12x15 inches. Sprinkle with Parmesan cheese. Then top with mozzarella cheese. From the smaller end, carefully roll meat (jelly roll fashion). Seal ends to keep cheese inside. Put on a baking rack or broiler pan and bake 1 hour at 350 degrees. Combine remaining tomato sauce and Italian seasonings. Spread all over meat loaf and cook 10 minutes longer. Serves 6-8

* Note: Add tomato sauce a little at a time.

Oriental Pancake

Michele Manya Buckley, St. Louis Parish, Clarksville

2 eggs or Egg Beaters
1/2 cup flour
1/2 cup skim milk
4 tablespoons sugar

1 teaspoon vanilla
Dash of nutmeg
2 tablespoons margarine

Melt margarine in a baking dish. Mix all the above ingredients, except the margarine in a blender. Pour mixture into the baking dish with the melted margarine. Bake for 20 minutes at 425 degrees. Cut pancake into square pieces and serve with yogurt or fruit preserves on top.

Pasta Primavera With Dijon

Sharon O' Donnell, Severna Park

1 pound sea shell macaroni, cooked
1 bunch green onions, chopped
2 large fresh tomatoes, diced
1 cup safflower oil
1/2 cup olive oil

1/2 cup cider vinegar
1 teaspoon Dijon mustard
Dash of garlic powder
Salt and pepper to taste

Toss macaroni with greens, onions and tomatoes. Combine oils, vinegar and Dijon; pour enough over pasta to moisten. Season. Serve hot or cold.

Pasta With Fresh Tomatoes

Sharon O' Donnell, Severna Park

7 ripe tomatoes, cut into 1/2 inch chunks
1 cup fresh basil leaves, chopped
2 tablespoons chopped fresh parsley
3 large cloves garlic, minced
3/4 teaspoon red pepper, crushed
1/8 teaspoon salt
1 pound low-fat Mozzarella cheese, cubed
1/3 cup safflower oil
1 pound sea shell-shaped pasta

Combine tomatoes, basil, parsley, garlic, red pepper, salt, cheese, safflower oil and olive oil. Let stand for one hour at room temperature. Cook pasta, drain; toss with tomatoes while still hot.

Broil, bake, steam or poach and avoid pan-frying or deep-frying.

Pork Chops With Cabbage

Patricia Richardson, St. Ursula Parish, Parkville

4 pork chops, cut 3/4 inch thick
1/2 cup water
3 cups shredded cabbage
2 tablespoons vinegar
1 tablespoon Dijon-style mustard
1-1/2 teaspoons sugar
1/8 teaspoon caraway seed
2 small green apples, cored and cut into thin wedges
1/3 cup light or dark raisins
1/8 teaspoon salt
Dash of pepper

Trim excess fat from pork chops. Place chops on an unheated rack of a broiler pan. Broil 5 inches from heat for 20-25 minutes or until no longer pink. Turn once. Meanwhile in a large saucepan bring water to boil. Add cabbage. Cook uncovered for about 3 minutes or until tender. Drain, return cabbage to saucepan. In a mixing bowl gradually combine vinegar and mustard. Stir in sugar, caraway seed, salt and pepper. Add apples and raisins. Toss and blend well. Cover and cook for 2-3 minutes or until apples are crisp. Serve pork chops over the cabbage mixture.

Pork Chops Pasquale

Father Paschal Morlino, OSB, Pastor, St. Benedict Parish, Baltimore

8 pork chops, trimmed
3 green peppers
3 medium onions
2 medium cans crushed tomatoes

2 cloves garlic, chopped
1 cup white wine
Italian spices (use over pork chops)

Broil pork chops lightly and place on large baking dish or pan. Place chopped green peppers and onions over pork chops. Pour the contents of both cans of crushed tomatoes into bowl and mash by hand. Pour tomato mixture over pork chops. Add wine and top with garlic. Bake uncovered at 350 degrees for 1-1/4 hours or until pork chops are tender.

Stuffed Pork Chops

Mary Lou Harper, Church of the Nativity, Timonium

6 double pork chops (cut for stuffing)
1 box Rice-a-Roni with almonds
2 apples, chopped and peeled
1/2 cup white raisins
1 cup apple juice
2 tablespoons butter, or margarine, melted

Simmer apples and raisins in apple juice until apples are tender. Drain and save juice. Prepare Rice-a-Roni according to pkg. directions. Combine rice, apples, and raisins. Stuff generously into pork chops. Brush chops with butter or margarine and put into a 9x12 inch pan. Pour 1/2 of apple juice over chops. Cover with foil and bake at 350 degrees for 30 minutes. Uncover and pour remaining juice and bake an additional 30 minutes.

Jenny's Pork Chops in Sour Cream

Joan Anne Rubis, St. Mary's Parish, Annapolis

5-6 center cut 1/2 inch thick pork chops, trimmed of fat
1/2 cup flour
2 tablespoons olive oil
5-6 whole cloves
1 cup sour cream, regular or low-fat
1-1/2 tablespoons sugar
2-1/2 tablespoons white wine vinegar
3/4 cup water
1-2 bay leaves

Rub chops with flour and brown in hot olive oil. Drain on paper towel. Push a whole clove into bony portion of each chop. Place pork chops in covered casserole. Combine remaining ingredients, except bay leaf. Place bay leaves on top of chops. Pour sour cream sauce over all. Cover and bake at 350 degrees for 1-1/4 hours or until chops are tender. Serves 5-6

Salmon Fusilli

Patricia Richardson, St. Ursula Parish, Parkville

1 (6 ounce package) fusilli or fettuccine
2 cups broccoli florets
1 (12 ounce can) skinless, boneless salmon, drained
1 tablespoon margarine
4 teaspoons cornstarch
1 cup skim milk
1/2 teaspoon dried tarragon, crushed
1/4 teaspoon lemon juice
Parsley (optional)
Pepper (optional)

Cook pasta and broccoli for 10 minutes or till tender. Drain, add salmon. In a medium saucepan, melt margarine. Blend in cornstarch. Add milk, bouillon granules and tarragon. Cook and stir till mixture is thickened and bubbly. Cook for 2 minutes more. Remove from heat. Stir in lemon juice. Spoon sauce over pasta mixture. Sprinkle with snipped parsley and pepper, if desired.

Succulent Scallops with Mushrooms

Pat Blakely, Timonium

1/2 pound sea scallops, sliced in half
Salt to taste
1/8 teaspoon pepper
1 tablespoon of margarine
2 cups mushrooms, sliced
2 tablespoons pine nuts, toasted
2 tablespoons minced shallots
1 garlic clove, minced
1/3 cup dry wine
2 tablespoons fresh lemon juice
2 cups hot cooked angel hair pasta(may use rice)

Sprinkle scallops with salt and pepper. Melt margarine in large non-stick skillet and add scallops, mushrooms, and pine nuts. Stir-fry 2 minutes. Remove scallop mixture from skillet. Set aside and keep warm. Add shallots and garlic to skillet and heat on low 30 seconds or until heated. Stir in wine and lemon juice. bring to boil and cook 2 minutes. Add scallop mixture to skillet and cook until thoroughly heated. Pour mixture over pasta or rice.

Seafood Strata

Barbara Hand, Baltimore

1 pound crabmeat (carefully cleaned)
1/4 teaspoon salt
3 shakes of paprika
1 tablespoon lemon juice
12 slices bread, remove crusts
12 slices Old English Cheese
4 eggs
2 cups half and half
6 tablespoons dry sherry

Butter bread and put 6 slices, butter down in 13x9 inch pan. Place a piece of cheese on each slice of bread. Cover with crab mixture and top with a second piece of cheese. Place remaining 6 slices of bread over crab, butter side up. In a bowl mix eggs and milk and pour over bread. Cover with plastic overnight in refrigerator. Remove 1/2 hour before baking. Bake at 325 degrees for 1 hour. Let stand 15 minutes before serving. Cut into 6 servings.

Remember nuts are high in fat and calories. (There is more fat in 1/2 cup of nuts than in a 3-ounce package of cream cheese.)

Shrimp Creole

Lisa Goodwin, St. William of York Parish, Baltimore

1/2 cup onion, diced
1/4 cup green pepper, diced
1/2 cup celery, diced
1/2 cup tomato juice
1 package Sweet N' Low
1/2 teaspoon salt
1/2 teaspoon Old Bay Seasoning
1 tablespoon parsley
1 bay leaf
1 (pound can) bean sprouts
1 (4 ounce can) mushrooms, drained
1 pound shrimp
1/2 teaspoon Worcestershire sauce

Sauté onion, green peppers, celery in tomato juice till tender. Add sweetener, salt, pepper, parsley, bay leaf, bean sprouts and Old Bay Seasoning. Cook gently for about 20 minutes. Remove bay leaf. Add mushrooms and shrimp. Heat until shrimp is cooked.

Spaghetti With Basil, Pine Nuts and Cheese

Patricia Richardson, St. Ursula Parish, Parkville

1 (8 ounce package) spaghetti
1 tablespoon virgin olive oil
1 garlic clove, crushed
1 cup basil leaves, shredded
1/2 cup unsalted chicken broth
1/4 cup pine nuts, toasted in small, dry skillet
1/2 cup fresh grated Romano
1/4 teaspoon salt
Fresh ground pepper

To prepare sauce, first pour the oil into a skillet and cook over medium heat. When oil is hot, add the garlic and cook stirring constantly for at least 30 seconds. Reduce heat to low. Stir in the basil and allow them to wilt. Pour in the stock and simmer gently, while you cook the pasta. Drain pasta and add to skillet with basil. Toss well to coat pasta. Add the pine nuts, cheese, salt and pepper. Mix well. Serve warm.

Spaghetti and Spinach Casserole

Pamela Gloss, St. John's Severna Park, Severna Park

1 (8 ounce package) spaghetti, cooked
1 small package frozen chopped spinach
1 egg
1 cup (8 ounce) non-fat yogurt
1/4 cup Parmesan cheese
1/2 teaspoon garlic
1 (8 ounce package) Monterey Jack shredded cheese
1 can Durkee Fried Onions

Combine egg, Parmesan cheese, and garlic. Thaw frozen spinach and drain well. Combine egg, cheese, and garlic mixture with noodles, spinach, and Monterey Jack with 1/2 can of dried onions. Bake in 1-1/2 quart baking dish. Top with the other half of onions. Bake at 350 degrees for 25 minutes.

Onion-Garlic Steak

Peggy Martin, Sacred Heart Church, Glyndon

Minced onion   Garlic powder
Soy sauce   Steak

*All quantities of ingredients vary depending on number and size of steaks.

Mix minced onion and garlic with soy sauce and brush over steak. Broil 8-12 minutes on each size.

Tuna Broccoli Casserole

Gerry Staib, St. Joseph Parish, Fullerton

2 eggs, beaten
1/2 cup skim milk (or 3/8 cup low-fat)
1 can tuna, packed in water
1 cup cottage cheese, small curd
1 (10 ounce package) chopped broccoli, thawed and drained
1/4 cup onion, chopped
1/4 teaspoon salt
Parmesan cheese

In bowl combine eggs, milk, tuna, cottage cheese, onion, salt and broccoli. Place in 9 inch pan. Bake at 350 degrees for 35 minutes. Remove from oven and sprinkle with Parmesan cheese. Return to oven for 10 minutes or until knife placed in center comes out clean.

Tuna Patties

Joan Anne Rubis, St. Mary's Parish, Annapolis

3 cans tuna, packed in water
1/2 cup bread crumbs
1/2 cup celery, chopped
3 large egg whites
2 tablespoons chopped onion
1 tablespoon chili powder
1/3 cup low-fat mayonnaise

Mix all ingredients together. Shape into cakes. Broil until light brown. Turn and broil on other side. Serve with salad, hot rolls and a light dessert.

Ginger Turkey Meatballs

Doris Dannenfelser, Baltimore

1 cup finely chopped onion
2 cloves garlic, minced
1 teaspoon ground ginger
1 teaspoon chili powder
1 pound ground turkey, made into meatballs
1 can whole tomatoes, undrained
1 cup water
2 teaspoons beef flavor bouillon cubes

Combine all ingredients and cook over slow heat and let simmer for about 1-1/2 hours.

Zucchini Crab Cakes

Mrs. Sam Curry, St. Francis of Assisi, Brunswick

2 cups zucchini, peeled and grated
1 cup Italian breadcrumbs
2 tablespoons Old Bay Seasoning
Dash of onion salt
1 egg
1 tablespoon Worcestershire Sauce

Peel and grate zucchini. In a medium bowl, add all ingredients and mix. Shape into small croquettes and chill. Fry in 1/2 inch of oil.

Tastes just like crabs!

Vegetables

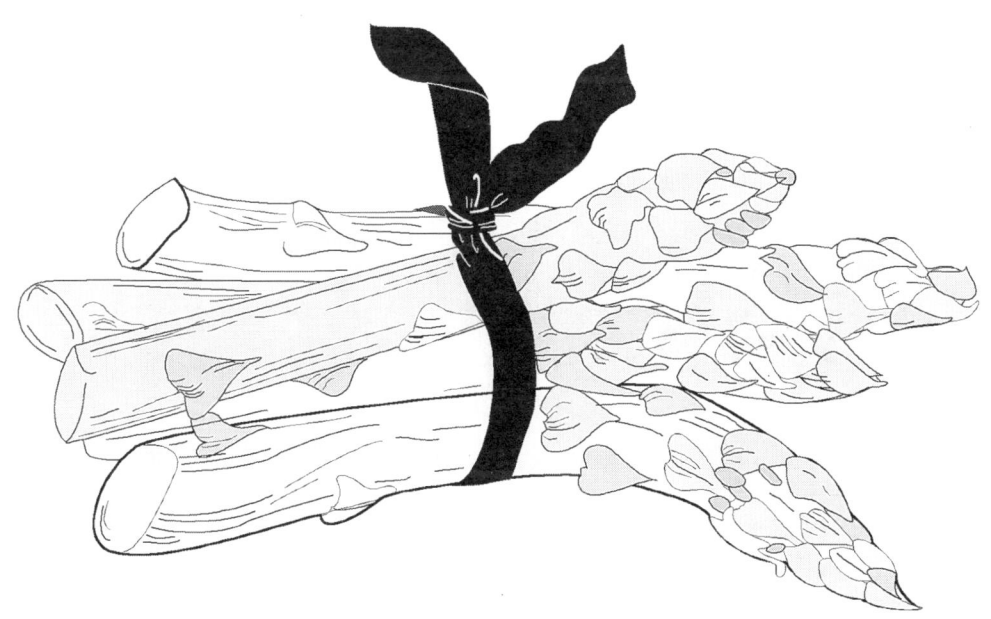

Lima Beans and Minted Peas

Katherine Olson, St. Paul Church, Ellicott City

1 cup fresh lima beans (may use frozen)
1 cup fresh peas (may use frozen)
1 cup pearl onions
4 tablespoons margarine or butter
2 teaspoons lemon juice
2 tablespoons chopped fresh mint.

In medium saucepan, cook lima beans in a small amount of boiling water. Cook about 8 minutes. Add peas and onions. Cook an additional 5 minutes or until beans are tender. Drain. Add margarine, lemon juice and mint. Toss gently. Garnish with fresh mint and lemons if desired. Makes 5 1/2 servings.

Christmas Broccoli

Patricia Eiberle Easter, St. Francis de Sales, Abingdon

3 bunches fresh broccoli
1 cup cider vinegar
1 tablespoon sugar
1 tablespoon Accent Seasoning

1 teaspoon salt
1 teaspoon pepper
1 teaspoon garlic pepper
1-1/2 teaspoons light oil

Cut broccoli into small florets. Mix remaining ingredients and pour over broccoli. Refrigerate overnight (at least 24 hours). Drain. Shape into round wreath. Use pimento for bow.

Orange-Sauced Broccoli

Patricia A. Richardson, St. Ursula Parish, Parkville

1 pound broccoli
1 medium red or yellow sweet pepper
2 tablespoons finely chopped onion
1 clove garlic, minced

1 tablespoon margarine
1-1/2 teaspoons cornstarch
2/3 cup orange juice
2 teaspoons (Dijon-style) mustard

Cut broccoli stalks lengthwise into spears. Cut pepper into 1-inch pieces. In a medium saucepan, cook broccoli and pepper in a small amount of boiling water for 8-10 minutes or until broccoli is crisp-tender. Drain and keep warm. In a saucepan, cook onions and garlic in hot margarine until onions are tender. Stir in cornstarch. Add orange juice and mustard. Cook and stir until mixture is thickened and bubbly. Cook for 2 minutes more. Spoon sauce over broccoli and pepper.

"My Best Bouquet" Brandied Carrots

Joan Anne Rubis, St. Mary's Parish, Annapolis

1 pound whole baby carrots
1/4 cup melted butter
1/4 cup brandy or pineapple juice

1 teaspoon brown sugar
1/4 teaspoon salt

Arrange carrots in an ungreased 8x8 inch pan. Mix remaining ingredients and pour over carrots. Cover and bake in a 375 degree oven for about 40 minutes or until carrots are tender. Uncover and bake an additional 15 minutes.

Judy's Herb "Bundle of Carrots"

Joan Anne Rubis, St. Mary's Parish, Annapolis

1 bundle (1-1/2 pounds) baby carrots
1/4 teaspoon salt
1/4 cup melted margarine
1/2 teaspoon thyme

1/2 teaspoon basil
1/4 teaspoon celery salt
1 teaspoon fresh orange juice

Steam sliced baby carrots until tender. Add margarine and other ingredients. Stir well and keep warm until ready to serve.

Our once tiny "carrot top" daughter Judy loved the little book called My Bundle of Carrots almost as much as she enjoyed this carrot recipe.

Honey Carrots

Jo Ann M. Nuetzel, Immaculate Heart of Mary, Baynesville

2/3 cup honey
2 tablespoons vegetable oil
1 teaspoon lemon juice
1/2 teaspoon salt (optional)
1 can carrot slices (may use fresh)

In a non- stick saucepan cook and stir honey, oil, juice and salt until bubbly. Add carrots. Cook on low heat stirring occasionally for 2-3 minutes. Serve warm.

Roasted Eggplant

Patti Medinger, Church of Nativity, Timonium

1 medium eggplant, cut into cubes
1 cup green pepper, cut in 1 inch slices
1 cup red pepper, cut in 1 inch slices
1 large sweet onion, cut into 8 wedges
1 garlic clove, minced
1 tablespoon olive oil
Salt and pepper
1 teaspoon ground cumin
2 tablespoons of red wine vinegar
1/8 teaspoon red pepper
1 tablespoon of parsley, chopped
 Cooking spray

Preheat oven to 400 degrees. Combine eggplant, green pepper, onion and garlic in shallow roasting pan. Drizzle oil over vegetables. Sprinkle with salt and pepper and toss well. Bake at 400 degrees for 45 minutes or until tender, stirring occasionally. Spoon eggplant mixture into a medium saucepan and set aside. Lightly spray a medium skillet with oil and sauté cumin over medium heat, for 20 seconds. Add cumin, wine vinegar, and red pepper to eggplant mixture and mix well. Sprinkle with parsley. Serve warm with French bread.

Honey Baked Figs

Lori Simmons, Cathedral of Mary Our Queen, Baltimore

12 dried figs
1/3 cup honey
2 tablespoons slivered almonds, toasted

Preheat oven to 325 degrees. Place figs in saucepan. Add water to cover and bring to boil. Cover, reduce heat and simmer 20 minutes. Remove from heat and let stand uncovered for 20 minutes. Drain well. Place figs in 1-1/2 quart baking dish. Drizzle with honey. Bake at 325 degrees for 25 minutes or until thoroughly heated, stirring occasionally. Sprinkle with toasted almonds. Serve warm.

This is a wonderful treat for the Holidays!

Potatoes Dalphinois

Martha Calabrese, Church of the Resurrection, Ellicott City

3 cups half and half
1/2 cup margarine
2 (12 ounce packages) frozen hash browns (thawed)
1/2 cup grated parmesan cheese

Heat cream and margarine together. Place thawed potatoes in a thin layer in a 9X13 inch pan. Pour cream mixture over potatoes. Sprinkle top with cheese. Bake at 325 degrees for an hour. Serves 8.

This recipe is great for taking to pot luck suppers.

Maryland Stewed Tomatoes

Marge Crossin, Holy Spirit Church, Joppatowne

1 pound can chopped tomatoes
1/2 cup dark brown sugar
1/2 cup melted butter or margarine
1/4 teaspoon salt
1 cup dry white bread (cut into 1 inch squares)
1/3 cup bread crumbs
1/3 cup Parmesan Plus

Drain tomatoes. Add sugar, butter, salt, dry bread and Parmesan Plus. Bake uncovered for 30 minutes at 375 degrees. 6 servings.

Summer Squash Delight

Father Paschal Morlino, OSB, Pastor, St. Benedict Parish, Baltimore

3 medium yellow squash, chopped
3 medium zucchini squash, chopped
3 onions, chopped
1 green pepper, chopped

6 eggs
1 clove garlic, minced
4 tablespoons olive oil

Sauté garlic and oil in skillet over low heat until lightly browned. Remove garlic from pan. Place chopped vegetables in skillet and simmer stirring often. Add salt and pepper to taste. Crack eggs into empty spaces of vegetables and cover until eggs are completely cooked. Serve on bed of pasta or greens.

"Corny" Tomato Salsa

Ron Price, St. Margaret Parish, Bel Air

4 ears of corn
Cooking spray
1/2 teaspoon ground cumin
1/4 teaspoon salt
1 garlic clove, minced
1/4 cup lime juice
1 cup red onions, sliced thick
1/2 teaspoon ground pepper
2-1/2 cups chopped tomato
3/4 cup sliced green onion

Cook corn completely and allow to cool before removing kernels. In a medium skillet, sauté onions on low heat until lightly browned, remove from heat and chop onions into smaller pieces. Let cool. Add remaining ingredients to cooled corn in a large bowl. Add cooled onions to mixture. Serve at room temperature or slightly chilled, with tortilla chips or tortilla shells.

When baking, you may substitute low-fat or regular plain yogurt for part or all of the sour cream.

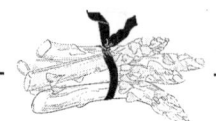

Notes

Desserts

Cakes
Cookies
Pastries
Puddings & Pies
Sweet Somethings

*C*akes

Fried Egg Dessert

(Angel Food Cake)

Patricia Eiberle Easter, St. Francis de Sales, Abingdon

Angel food cake, sliced
1 large can peach, halved (may use fresh)
Cool whip

Take a slice of angel food cake and place in center of dessert plate. Spread cool whip over cake slice. Place one peach slice in center of cool whip.

I had a birthday party for my mom and I told the ladies at the party I was going to serve a fried egg dessert. They didn't say much, but when I returned with the tray of desserts they all agreed they looked just like fried eggs! The best part is this tasty dessert is low in calories.

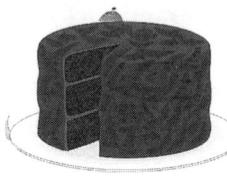

Maryland Black Walnut Cake

Patricia V. Saunders, St. Ursula Parish, Parkville

2 cups sifted flour
2-3/4 teaspoons baking powder
1/4 teaspoon salt
2/3 cup shortening
1-1/2 cups sugar
1 teaspoon vanilla
3 eggs, separated
3/4 cup milk
1-1/2 cups ground black walnuts

Sift flour, baking powder and salt. Cream shortening with sugar and vanilla until fluffy. Add beaten egg yolks and beat thoroughly. Add sifted dry ingredients and milk alternately in small amounts to sugar and egg mixture. Add nuts. Fold in beaten egg whites. Pour into two greased 9 inch cake pans. Bake in preheated 350 degree oven for 30 minutes.

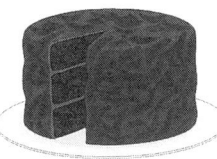

Cassata Alla Siciliana

(Sicilian Cake with Chocolate Frosting)

Rosalinda Mannetta-Poma, St. Leo the Great, Little Italy

1 pound cake
1 pound fresh ricotta cheese
2 tablespoons heavy cream
1/4 cups sugar
3 tablespoons Strega Liqueur or any orange-flavored liqueur
3 tablespoons mixed candied fruit, chopped
1/4 cup semi-sweet chocolate, chopped

With a sharp knife, slice ends off of the pound cake, and level top. Cut the cake horizontally into 1/2 inch thick slabs. In a mixing bowl, beat ricotta until smooth. Beating constantly, add the cream, sugar and Strega Liqueur. With a rubber spatula, fold in the candied fruit and chocolate. Place bottom slab of cake on a flat plate and spread generously with ricotta mixture. Place another slab on the top and repeat until all slabs and ricotta are used up, ending with cake. Gently press the loaf to make it compact. Refrigerate for 2 hours or until ricotta is firm.

Chocolate Frosting

Rosalinda Mannetta-Poma, St. Leo the Great, Little Italy

1 (12 ounce package) semi-sweet chocolate, chopped into small pieces
3/4 cup of strong black espresso coffee
1/2 pound unsalted butter, cut into 1/2 inch pieces (thoroughly chilled)

Melt chocolate with coffee in a small heavy saucepan over low heat, stirring constantly until chocolate has completely dissolved. Remove from heat and beat in chilled butter, one piece at a time until the mixture is smooth. Chill until spreading consistency is reached. With a metal spatula, frost cake evenly. Refrigerate at least one day before serving.

Serve with espresso coffee for a perfect ending to a good meal.

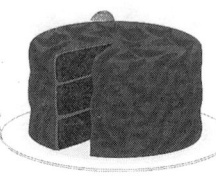

Swirled Cheesecake

Joan Anne Rubis, St. Mary's Parish, Annapolis

3 (8 ounce packages) cream cheese
1 cup granulated sugar
1 cup sour cream (low-fat)
1 tablespoon vanilla
2 eggs, large or (4 egg whites)
1/4 cup semi-sweet chocolate, melted

Crust:
1 cup chocolate wafers, crushed (about 18)
1 tablespoon margarine, melted

In small bowl combine margarine and crushed wafer crumbs. Stir well. Press into bottom of 8 or 9 inch spring form pan.

In large mixing bowl, combine softened cream cheese and sugar for 2 minutes. Beat in sour cream, flour and vanilla. Add eggs one at a time, beating well after each. Pour 1-1/2 cups of batter to a small bowl and stir in melted chocolate. Spread half of vanilla batter over the crust. Gently pour half of chocolate batter on top. Spoon rest of vanilla batter over the chocolate batter and chocolate batter on top. Swirl batter together with a knife. In a shallow roasting pan place cheesecake pan and then add enough boiling water to come halfway up cheesecake pan. Bake in a 325 degree oven for 1 hour and 15 minutes. Remove pan and place on rack to cool. Cover and chill for about 4 hours or overnight.

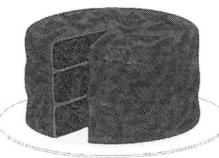

Dirt Cake

Marge Crossin, Holy Spirit Parish, Joppatowne

1/4 cup margarine, softened
1/2 cup confectioners sugar
1 (8 ounce package) light cream cheese, softened
1 (12 ounce container) whipped topping
2 (4 ounce packages) vanilla instant pudding
3-1/2 cups skim milk
1 (16 ounce package) Oreo sandwich cookies

Cream margarine, confectioners sugar and cream cheese until light and fluffy. Combine whipped topping, pudding mix and milk and mix well. Combine with creamed mixture. Crush cookies. Place cookie crumbs in bottom of a clean clay pot that has been lined with saran wrap. Alternate layers of cream mixture and cookie crumbs, ending with a heavy layer of cookie crumbs. Place a few gummy worms sticking out of crumbs. May decorate with artificial flowers. Chill until serving time.

This is a fun dessert to serve at a picnic or for a children's birthday party. I purchased new garden tools and after sterilizing them I used the tools for serving. I know your family and friends will enjoy this dessert!

Pineapple Banana Cake

Brother Kevin Strong, FSC, President Calvert Hall College, Baltimore

3 cups flour
1 teaspoon baking soda
1 teaspoon cinnamon
2 cups sugar
1 teaspoon salt
1-1/2 cups oil
3 eggs
1-1/2 teaspoons vanilla
2 cups ripe bananas
1 (8 ounce can) crushed pineapple

Combine all dry ingredients and set aside. Dice the bananas and add to dry mixture. Add oil, vanilla, eggs and crushed pineapple (do not drain). Stir together but do not use beater. Pour into greased and floured tube pan. Bake at 350 degrees for one hour and twenty minutes. Cake will be moist. Let cool in the pan.

Use unsweetened plain cocoa powder instead of baking chocolate whenever possible. Use "dark" carob powder for even less fat. Unlike cocoa, carob does not contain caffeine.

Plum or Peach Cake

Barbara Hand, Baltimore

2 cups flour
4 teaspoons baking powder
6 tablespoons sugar
Pinch of salt

Add: (to above mixture)

1/3 cup shortening
1 large egg beater
2/3 cup milk

Spread dough into a greased roll pan (7x12x1-1/2 inches deep). Cover dough with fresh plums or peaches. Add cream mixture.*

Cream*
1/4 cup soft butter
1/4 cup sugar
3 tablespoons flour

Drop creamed mixture on top of fruit. Bake at 400 degrees for 35-40 minutes. Sprinkle with powdered sugar and serve warm..

Peach and Caramel Shortcake

Mary Donnally, St. Joseph Parish, Hagerstown

1/4 cup margarine
1/2 cup brown sugar, firmly packed
1 tablespoon light corn syrup
1/4 cup whipped cream
Short cake or 4 sponge cake cups
2 peaches, sliced
1/4 cup whipped cream

Melt margarine in small saucepan and stir in brown sugar and corn syrup. Bring to boil. Cook until sugar is dissolved, stirring constantly. Remove from heat. Beat in whipped cream. To serve, place sponge cake cup on 4 separate plates. Top each with peach slices, drizzle caramel sauce over peaches and top with whipped cream.

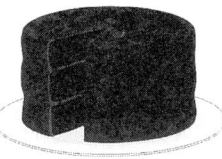

Sugar Cakes

Ruth E. Topper, St. Edmond's Parish, Rehoboth Beach

2 cups sugar
1 cup Crisco
3 eggs (beaten)
1 cup buttermilk
1 teaspoon vanilla
1 teaspoon soda
3-1/2 cups flour
1 teaspoon baking powder
1/2 teaspoon salt

Mix sugar, Crisco and beaten eggs. Blend buttermilk, vanilla and soda and add to sugar mixture. Add remaining ingredients and mix thoroughly. Drop on greased cookie sheet and press with sugared glass. Bake in a 400 degree oven for 8 to10 minutes.

All Eyes On Carrot Cake

Patti Medinger, Church of Nativity, Timonium

2-1/2 cups flour
1-1/2 teaspoons baking powder
1/2 teaspoon salt
1 teaspoon cinnamon
4 eggs, separated
1-1/2 cups vegetable oil

2-1/2 cups sugar
1/3 cup hot water
1-1/2 cups grated carrots
1 teaspoon fresh lemon juice
1 cup walnuts, chopped

Preheat oven to 350 degrees. Grease two 9x5 inch loaf pans with butter or shortening and dust with flour. Sift together flour, baking powder, soda, salt and cinnamon. Set aside. Separate eggs. In a large bowl, beat oil, sugar, hot water and egg yolks with an electric mixer until creamy. Add carrots and nuts. Beat the egg whites with fresh lemon juice until they form stiff peaks. Fold half the whites into the batter and mix thoroughly. Fold in remaining whites gently until no lumps of white can be seen. Divide mixture into two prepared pans. Bake for 60 to 75 minutes or until firm when pressed on.

Glaze

3/4 cup powdered sugar
1 tablespoon fresh lemon juice
1/4 cup grated carrots

Beat above ingredients until creamy. Drizzle over cakes while they are still warm.

This recipe is not a light recipe, but will be enjoyed by all for any occasion. I got it from the cookbook "Chicken Soup For The Soul" which was given to me by a special friend. This carrot cake recipe had been a favorite in her family as well!

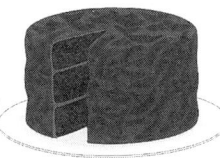

Fudge Cake

Tom Blakery, Baltimore

2 cups margarine or butter, (may use half of each)
2 cups flour
1 teaspoon baking soda
2 cups sugar
1/2 cup cocoa
2 large eggs, beaten
1/2 cup low-fat sour cream
1 teaspoon almond extract
1/4 teaspoon salt
1 cup water

Preheat oven to 350 degrees. In a saucepan, add cocoa, water, and butter and bring to boil. Set aside. Sift all dry ingredients together and add to hot mixture. Add beaten eggs, sour cream, and almond extract to mixture. Pour into prepared 13x9 inch lightly greased pan. Bake for 30 minutes or until it feels firm in the center.

Glaze

1/2 stick margarine, softened
3 tablespoon cocoa
1/4 cup milk
1 teaspoon almond extract
2 cups powdered sugar (add gradually for desired consistency)

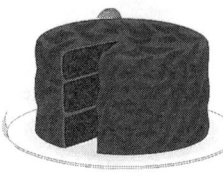

Wine Cake

Kathy Kelly, St. John the Evangelist, Hydes

1 pkg. yellow cake mix
1 pkg. instant vanilla pudding
1 teaspoon nutmeg
4 eggs
3/4 cup Riunite Blush Bianco
3/4 cup oil
Ground almonds (optional)

Place all ingredients in large bowl and beat 5 minutes or until batter is very smooth. Butter angel cake pan generously. (Optional...for a gourmet touch, dust the buttered pan with ground almonds.) Bake in a 350 degree oven for 55 minutes. Place upright on rack for 5 minutes to cool; turn out and dust with powdered sugar. Best when allowed to mellow for 2-3 days before serving.

This is an excellent cake for an adult birthday party. The first time I served this cake was for six adults after a delicious Italian dinner. It is the only cake I can remember being completely eaten on the first day it was served. It's that good! You just keep nibbling until it's all gone.

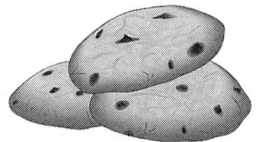

Cookies

Corn Flake Crispies

Catherine Macy, Catholic Community of St. Michael/ St. Patrick, Baltimore

1 cup margarine (2 sticks)
1 cup granulated sugar
1 teaspoon baking soda
1 teaspoon cream of tartar
1-1/2 cups flour
2 cups corn flakes, crumbled

Blend in order given. Mix well. Drop by teaspoon on ungreased cookie sheet. Flatten with fork. Bake 350 degrees for 10-15 minutes.

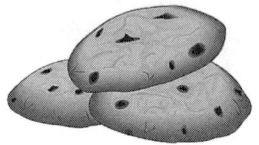

Kolachy (Cookie)

Jean Kovalic Barczak, St. Ursula Parish, Parkville

1 cup butter
1/2 teaspoon salt
1 (8 ounce package) cream cheese

1/4 teaspoon vanilla
2-1/4 cups flour

Cream butter, salt and cream cheese. Add vanilla and then flour. Chill for a few hours or overnight in refrigerator. Roll out pieces of dough and cut into squares. Spread some filling* to just short of the edge of the dough. Roll diagonally. Preheat oven to 375 degrees. Bake for about 12 minutes or until lightly brown on a ungreased cookie sheet

*Filling

1 pound walnut meat
1/2 quart milk
1 cup sugar
1/4 pound margarine

Mix above ingredients in saucepan and bring to boil. Mixture is ready when it becomes thick and is spreadable. Let cool. Spread on cookie dough.

These nut roll cookies are a family favorite from my father's side of the family. A lot of work, but well worth your time. You can also use the nut filling in your bread recipes. Once your dough has risen, spread out and cover with nut filling. Roll up loaf and brush with beaten egg and bake.

The nut bread was a tradition for Christmas and Easter. My father had a knack with the bread dough and could really get that dough to rise. He'd get up sometimes at 5 a.m. to "punch" that dough. No one could make nut bread like he could!

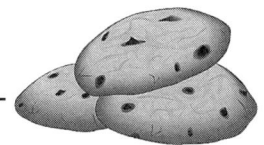

Giant Oatmeal Cookies

Ann H. Gunning, St. John the Evangelist, Hydes

1 cup butter
1 cup sugar
1 cup firmly packed brown sugar
2 eggs
1 teaspoon vanilla
1-1/2 cups flour
2 teaspoons cinnamon
2 teaspoons ground allspice
1 teaspoon ground ginger
2 teaspoons ground cloves
1/2 teaspoon salt
1/2 teaspoon baking soda
3 cups quick-cooking oats

Cream butter, sugar and brown sugar until light and fluffy. Beat in eggs and vanilla. Stir together flour, cinnamon, allspice, cloves, ginger, salt and baking soda. Stir flour mixture into butter mixture. Stir in oats. Let dough sit at room temperature for 2 hours. Drop about 1/4 cup of dough at a time onto lightly greased cookie sheets. Flatten cookies slightly with the back of a spoon. Bake in 375 degree oven for 10 minutes. Do not overbake. Makes about two dozen large cookies. About six cookies will fit on each cookie sheet. Remove from oven when the cookie is still puffy and edges are just starting to turn light brown.

My father first "spied" this recipe in the Baltimore Sun on Sunday, August 8, 1979 and it has become a family favorite.

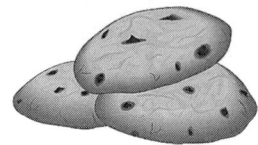

Raisin Filled Cookies

Genevieve Gorczyca Kovalic, Shrine of the Little Flower Parish, Baltimore

1-1/2 cups sugar
1 cup shortening
2 eggs
5 cups flour
2 teaspoons baking soda
4 teaspoons cream of tartar
Pinch of salt
2 teaspoons vanilla
1 cup milk

Cream sugar, shortening, and eggs. Cream together. Add vanilla. Add flour, salt, baking soda, and cream of tartar. Add milk. Refrigerate for 3 hours or overnight. Take 1/4 dough and roll out on floured surface. Cut with round cookie cutter. Fill rounds with 1 teaspoon of raisin filling. Cover with another circle of dough and seal all sides. Allow space between cookies on cookie sheet. Bake 18 minutes or until edges are lightly brown in a 350 degree oven.

Raisin Filling:

2 cups raisins
2 cups boiling water
1/2 cup sugar
3 tablespoons flour
3 tablespoons lemon juice

Place raisins and water in a pot and cook about 10 minutes or until tender. After raisins are boiled, mix the sugar and flour and add a little hot water from the raisins to the sugar and flour. Stir. Add a little more of the hot water to this mixture. Then pour into the hot raisins and boil about 1-2 minutes. Stir until it boils and thickens. Add lemon juice and stir. Let stand until it cools.

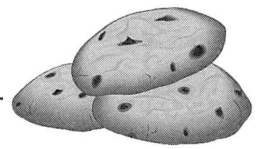

Old "Faithful" Sugar Cookie

Patti Medinger, Church of Nativity, Timonium

1 cup sweet butter (may use 1/2 margarine and 1/2 butter)
1-1/2 cups sugar
3 eggs (may substitute egg beaters)
1 teaspoon vanilla extract
4 cups flour
1 teaspoon baking powder
1/2 teaspoon baking soda
1/8 teaspoon salt
1 teaspoon cinnamon
1/4 teaspoon nutmeg
1 teaspoon cream of tartar

Cream butter with sugar until fluffy. Stir in eggs, one at a time. Beat well. Stir in vanilla. Sift flour with baking powder, soda, salt, cinnamon, cream of tartar, and nutmeg. Gradually add flour mixture to butter mixture. Chill mixture, cover overnight. Generously flour surface for rolling cookie dough.(May use bread board or kitchen counter.) Roll dough to about 1/8 inch thick and use cookie cutters for desired shapes. Bake on non-stick cookie sheets in a 375 degree oven for 8-10 minutes. Remove from oven when they begin to appear lightly brown...do not overbake. Makes about 4 dozen cookies.

Optional Frosting

4 cups powdered sugar
1 stick margarine, softened
1 teaspoon vanilla extract
Food coloring
Milk

Combine ingredients and blend using milk sparingly to obtain spreadable consistency. Divide frosting into 4 parts and add a drop of food coloring to each for decorating fun.

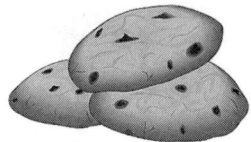

Vinegar Cookies

Jo Ann M. Nuetzel, Immaculate Heart of Mary, Baynesville

1 cup margarine
1 cup sugar
1-1/2 cups flour
1 tablespoon vinegar
1/2 teaspoon baking soda

Heat margarine and sugar at low speed. Add flour, vinegar and soda. Refrigerate one hour. Drop on ungreased cookie sheet. Bake in a 350 degree oven 15 minutes. Yields: 4 dozen

I received this recipe from a Sodality sister at a cookie exchange party this past Christmas season. The name of these cookies might make one hesitate to try them, but let me assure you these cookies are m-m-good!

Use non-stick vegetable spray.

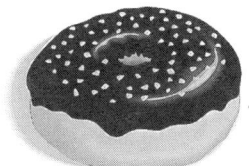

*P*astries

Scalloped Apples

Tracy Foot, Baltimore

6 large apples
1/4 teaspoon cinnamon
1/4 teaspoon salt
1 tablespoon lemon juice
1/4 cup water
3/4 cup sugar
1/4 cup flour
1/3 cup butter (may substitute margarine)

Pare, core and slice apples. Arrange apples in a shallow, greased baking dish. Mix cinnamon, salt, lemon juice and water. Pour mixture over apples. Mix sugar, flour and butter until crumbly and sprinkle on top. Bake in a 400 degree oven for 30 minutes or until apples are completely cooked.

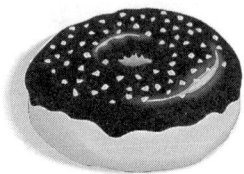

Tropical Fruit Napoleons

Teri Lynn Black, Severna Park

1/2 cup fat-free sour cream
1/3 cup sifted powdered sugar
1/3 cup soft tofu
1/4 cup light cream cheese
2 tablespoons dry bread crumbs
2 tablespoons granulated sugar
1/4 teaspoon ground cinnamon
5 sheets frozen phyllo
   dough, thawed
1/2 teaspoon lemon rind

2 tablespoons reduced-calorie
   stick margarine, melted
Cooking spray
1/2 cup diced carambola (star
   fruit) (optional fruits may
   be used)
1/2 cup diced peeled papaya
1/2 cup diced banana
1 tablespoon powdered sugar

Combine first five ingredients in a bowl and beat at medium speed. Cover and chill. Combine breadcrumbs, granulated sugar and cinnamon. Set aside. Preheat oven to 375 degrees. Place phyllo sheet on a large cutting board. Lightly brush margarine on surface. Sprinkle with 1 tablespoon breadcrumb mixture. Repeat layers with remaining phyllo, margarine, breadcrumb mixture ending with phyllo. Gently press phyllo layers together and lightly coat top with cooking spray. Cut 12 (3 inch) circles through phyllo layers using a sharp knife. Place layered circles on a greased baking sheet. Bake at 375 degrees for 12 minutes or until crisp. Cool completely. Combine carambola, papaya, and banana and stir gently. Place 1 phyllo stack on each of four dessert plates. Spread 1 tablespoon of sour cream mixture on top of each stack. Top with 3 tablespoon of papaya mixture and 1 tablespoon sour cream mixture. For each serving, repeat layer with the remaining phyllo stacks, sour cream mixture, and papaya mixture, ending with phyllo stacks. Sprinkle powdered sugar over napoleons.

I cut this recipe from a magazine this summer and I thought it would be a good choice for a low-fat and delicious treat. I made the recipe for my ladies card club and replaced the carambola (starfruit) with fresh raspberries...after the dessert we forgot who won the card game.

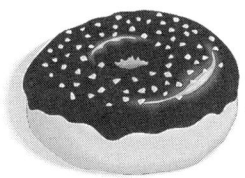

Golden Sunburst Tart

Helen C. Bridges, St. Patricks Parish, LaVale

1-1/2 cups sifted flour
1 teaspoon cream of tarter
1/2 teaspoon baking soda
1/4 teaspoon salt

1/2 cup butter or margarine
3/4 cup sugar
1 beaten egg
1/2 teaspoon vanilla

Sift together flour, cream of tarter, baking soda, and salt. Set aside. Cream together butter or margarine and sugar until fluffy, using electric mixer. Add beaten egg and vanilla to creamed butter mixture. Stir in dry ingredients and mix until crumbs form. Press mixture into a 12 inch pizza pan. Bake in a 350 degree oven for 20 minutes or until golden brown. Cool on rack.

Filling:

1 (8 ounce pkg). cream
   cheese, softened
1/2 cup sugar
2 teaspoons pineapple juice
1/4·cup sugar
4 teaspoons cornstarch

1 cup pineapple juice
10 red maraschino cherries, halved
1 medium banana, sliced
1 (8 ounce can) sliced peaches, drained
1 (8 ounce can) pineapple chunks, drained

Combine cream cheese, 1/2 cup sugar and 2 teaspoon of pineapple juice. Beat until smooth and creamy. Spread mixture over cooled cookie crust. Combine remaining sugar and cornstarch in small saucepan and cook over low to medium heat until mixture boils and becomes thick. Let cool while preparing fruit. Arrange apricots, cut side down and place around edge of crust. Place a cherry half between each apricot half. Form a ring of banana slices and then a ring of peach slices. Arrange pineapple chunks in center. Spoon cooled sauce evenly over fruit. Chill in refrigerator at least 2 hours. Makes 12-16 servings.

This recipe comes from a Kansas homemaker and is very nutritious. It may take a little time, but can be a fun activity to involve the kids in. There could be some pretty unique fruit designs!

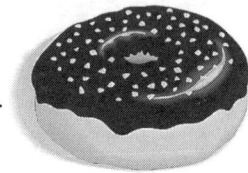

Notes

Puddings & Pies

Berry De-lite

Barbara Gloss, Olyphant, Pennsylvania

Crust
1- 1/2 cups graham cracker crumbs
1/4 cup sugar
1/3 cup melted margarine

Filling
1 (8 ounce container) low-fat cream cheese
1/4 cup sugar
2 tablespoons skim milk
1- 3/4 cups cool whip, thawed, low-fat
Fresh fruit (strawberries, blueberries, peaches)

Pudding
3-1/2 cups cold milk
2 (4 ounce packages) vanilla instant pudding

Combine ingredients for crust and press into a 9x13 inch pan and chill. Beat all ingredients for filling and spread over chilled crust. Arrange fresh fruit of your choice over top of mixture. Chill. Prepare pudding as directed on package. Pour over fresh fruit. Chill several hours before serving. Before serving spread 2 cups fat free cool whip over pudding. Garnish with additional fruit.

Old Fashioned Bread Pudding

Doris Dannenfelser, St. Margaret's Parish, Bel Air

6 slices day-old white bread (remove crust)
2 tablespoons reduced-calorie margarine, melted
3/4 cup sugar substitute
1 teaspoon ground cinnamon
1/2 cup seedless raisins
4 eggs, beaten
3 cups skim milk
1 teaspoon vanilla extract
Vegetable spray

Brush bread lightly with melted margarine. Sprinkle 1 teaspoon sugar substitute and cinnamon. Quarter each bread slice. Layer with raisins in a 1 1/2 quart casserole dish coated with vegetable spray. Set aside. Combine eggs, milk, vanilla and remaining sugar substitute. Pour over bread and raisins. Place dish in a pan containing 1 inch of hot water. Bake in a 350 degree oven for 1 hour or until a knife inserted in center comes out clean. Serve warm, or cover and refrigerate until thoroughly chilled.

Omit some yolks in cooking and baking and use extra whites instead. (Substitute 2 large egg whites for 1 large egg.)

Raspberry Bread Pudding

Diane Thompson-Griggs, Phoenix

2-1/2 pints of raspberries
1-1/2 teaspoons cornstarch
8 slices firm white bread
4 egg whites

2/3 cup sugar + 1 tablespoon
1-1/2 cups skim milk
1/2 teaspoon almond extract
Salt

Lightly grease a shallow 1-1/2 quart baking dish. Combine raspberries and cornstarch and spread in dish. Trim the crusts of the bread and toast bread. Spread one side of each piece of toast with some butter or margarine. Cut each piece in half to form a triangle. Arrange two layers of toast, buttered side up in prepared dish. Beat the egg whites and add the 2/3 cup sugar until light. Gradually beat in milk, almond extract and a pinch of salt until sugar dissolves. Slowly pour over the toast and fruit. Let stand 15 minutes. Heat oven to 325 degrees. Sprinkle top of pudding with remaining 1 tablespoon sugar. Put baking dish in a roasting pan and fill pan halfway with warm water to make a water bath. Bake until set, about 1 hour and 15 minutes.

Jell-O Dessert

Joan Anne Rubis, St. Mary's Parish, Annapolis

1 (4 ounce package) gelatin (any flavor)
1/2 cup powdered milk

Mix gelatin as directed on package. Put into refrigerator until syrupy (about 20 minutes). Then beat until frothy and nearly doubled in volume. Pour in 1/2 cup of powdered milk and continue beating until well blended. Spoon into 6-7 dessert dishes.

This is my most favorite and delicious "lose weight" dessert.

Watermelon and Blackberry Compote

Diane Thompson-Griggs

3/4 cup sugar
2 tablespoon chopped fresh mint
4 pounds watermelon (about 4 cups of watermelon chunks)
2 cup blackberries

In a saucepan, combine sugar and 3/4 cup water over medium heat. Cook, stirring occasionally, until sugar dissolves. Bring to a boil and cook until syrup thickens slightly and reduces to about 3/4 cup, about 5-7 minutes. Remove from heat. Stir in mint and refrigerate. Cut watermelon into chunks and combine with the blackberries and mint syrup.

$\mathcal{S}$weet $\mathcal{S}$omethings

Butterscotch Crunches

Elaine M. Carson, St. Edmond Parish, Rehoboth Beach

2 (6 ounce packages) Nestles butterscotch morsels (may use chocolate)
1 (3 ounce can) or (2 cups) chow mein noodles
1 cup salted peanuts

Melt butterscotch morsels over hot (not boiling) water. Remove from heat. Stir in chow mein noodles and salted peanuts. Drop by teaspoonfuls onto waxed paper. Let stand until set, approximately 20 minutes.

The RCIA classes at St. Edmond's often enjoyed treats made by the Core team members, catechumens and the candidates. Agnes Pasqualini shared the recipe with everyone at a church gathering one night. The butterscotch crunches were a big hit! This recipe is easy and requires no baking. I continue to make them for family and friends.

Diabetic Chocolate Fudge

Barbara Gloss, Olyphant, Pennsylvania

1 envelope unflavored gelatin
1/4 cup water
1 square unsweetened chocolate
1/8 teaspoon cinnamon

12 packs Equal
1/2 cup evaporated milk
1/4 cup water

Mix gelatin and water and set aside. Melt chocolate, cinnamon. Add sugar, evaporated milk, water to melted chocolate. Remove from stove and add vanilla. Cool. When mixture thickens add chopped nuts (optional). When firm, cut into squares.

A Peachy Delight

Massimiliano & Rosalinda Poma, St. Leo's Parish, Little Italy

Ripe peaches   Red wine

Slice peaches and place in wine glass. Pour wine over and chill while serving dinner. Serve as dessert.

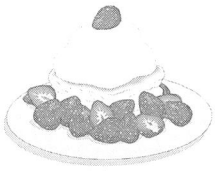

Dreamy Orange Delight

Sue Ebourly, Cathedral of Mary Our Queen, Baltimore

2 small boxes orange jello
2 cups boiling water
1 small can frozen orange juice concentrate
1 small can crushed pineapple, undrained
1 small can mandarin oranges, drained
1 orange (sliced thin) optional garnish

Melt orange jello with boiling water. When completely dissolved add frozen juice concentrate, crushed pineapple with juice and drained mandarin oranges. Pour into a glass bowl or container about 9x12. Refrigerate a few hours until mixture is well set.

Chiffon Topping
2 small boxes instant vanilla pudding
2 small bags of Dream whip
2 cups cold milk

Add vanilla pudding, dream whip, and cold milk to a small bowl. Beat until it is the consistency of a stiff frosting. Spread over top of jello. Garnish with thin slices of oranges.

Peach Dessert

Peche Cardinals

Brother Kevin Strong, FSC, President, Calvert Hall College, Baltimore

Marinate canned peach halves in raspberry liqueur. Serve in champagne glass with pureed raspberries and whipped topping. Garnish with shaved chocolate and a few whole raspberries.

Pineapple Casserole

Terry Leight, Baltimore

3 eggs*
3 tablespoons flour
1/2 cup sugar (optional)
Pinch of salt
1 (8 ounce can) pineapple chunks with juice
6 slices bread
1 stick margarine

Beat eggs, flour, sugar and salt until smooth. Add the pineapple (do not drain). Stir until blended. Cube bread and place on top of pineapple mixture. Melt the margarine and pour on top. Bake in a 350 degree oven for 45 minutes.

*Instead of eggs, substitute egg beaters

This recipe came to me from my Aunt Eve's parish cookbook from St Elizabeth's parish. It is one of those "what can I make that's different for dinner tonight?" I made it and served it as a side dish with ham. On another occasion I used it at a family gathering and served it as a dessert. Now when we go to family picnics or parties, I will ask what to bring....and they always say "bring that pineapple thing you make".

Cold Peach and Strawberry Delight

Melissa Januk, Baltimore

1 peeled peach, sliced
1 cup sliced strawberries
1 (8 ounce container) peach or strawberry yogurt
1-2 tablespoons sugar
2 tablespoons lemon juice
Lemon slices
Fresh mint sprigs

In blender, combine all ingredients except lemon slices and mint, until mixture is smooth. Pour into medium size dessert bowls and chill covered 1-2 hours. Garnish with lemon slice and mint sprig.

Note: Mixture has consistency of thick soup, and can be used for a refreshing dessert or as a beginning course to a meal. Serve with little cookies on the side.

Fruit Fantasia

Pam Silver, Cathedral of Mary Our Queen, Baltimore

1 large banana, peeled, sliced
1 pineapple, cut into chunks
1 peach, peeled, sliced
1 orange, peeled, sliced
1 cup of fresh raspberries or strawberries
1 mango, peeled, sliced
1 papaya, peeled, sliced

Place fruit on serving platter. For the dressing: Combine reserve peaches, 1 cup non-fat peach flavored yogurt and 2 tablespoon honey. Pour over fruit and serve.

Baked Fruit

Judy Meyer, Resurrection Parish, Catholic Daughters, State Treasurer

1 can pears
1 can peaches
1 can pineapple chunks
3-4 apples
4 bananas

1 box coconut cookies (hard)
1/4-1/2 cups Bourbon
1/4 pound butter
1/4 cup brown sugar

Cut peaches, pears into quarters. Peel apples, remove core; slice into quarters. Slice bananas 1 inch thick. Mix fruit together. Crumble 1/2 box cookies into fruit mixture. Mix well. Place in 13 x 9 inch casserole. Add liquid from fruit and bourbon. Dot top with butter. Sprinkle brown sugar over butter. Top with remainder of crushed cookies. Bake 300 degrees for 30 minutes.

Have a Heart

Recipes for the Heart Smart

Low-fat and Low-cholesterol Meals

Courtesy of the American Heart Association,
American Heart Association, National Heart Center

Breads

Gingerbread

1 cup dark molasses
1/2 cup firmly packed brown sugar
1/2 cup acceptable vegetable oil
1/2 teaspoon cinnamon
1/2 teaspoon nutmeg
1/2 teaspoon cloves
1 teaspoon ground ginger
1 cup boiling water
2-1/2 cups all-purpose flour, unsifted
1 teaspoon baking soda
2 tablespoons hot water

Preheat oven to 350 degrees. Lightly spray an 8 inch square pan with vegetable oil. In a large bowl, blend together molasses, brown sugar, oil and spices. Stir in boiling water. Mix in flour. Set aside. In a small bowl, dissolve baking soda in 2 tablespoon hot water. Stir well and add to batter. Bake in prepared pan 30 minutes. Remove from oven and slice into twelve equal portions. Serve warm.

Oat Bran Fruit Muffins

1-1/2 cups high fiber oat bran cereal
3/4 cup all-purpose flour
3/4 cup whole-wheat flour
2 teaspoons baking powder
1 teaspoon cinnamon
1/2 cup raisins
1/2 cup chopped dated
1/2 cup chopped prunes
1/4 cup firmly packed dark brown sugar
1 cup low-fat buttermilk
1/2 cup honey
3 tablespoons acceptable vegetable oil
2 eggs, well beaten

Preheat oven to 350 degrees. Line muffin tin with paper liners. In a large bowl, mix oat bran, flours, baking powder, baking soda, cinnamon and dried fruits. In another bowl, mix brown sugar, buttermilk, honey, oil and eggs. Make a well in dry ingredients. Pour liquid mixture into well and stir gently. Do not overmix. Spoon into paper-lined muffin tin. Bake 20-25 minutes.

Yogurt Dinner Rolls

1/4 cup warm water
2 tablespoons sugar
1 pkg. active dry yeast
1 cup plain nonfat yogurt
1 tablespoon acceptable margarine, melted
1 egg
1 teaspoon leaf oregano
2 teaspoons basil
2 tablespoons grated onion
3/4 cup all-purpose flour
3/4 cup whole-wheat flour
1/2 teaspoon salt
1/2 cup all-purpose flour
3/4 cup whole wheat flour
Vegetable oil spray

In a bowl, combine water, sugar, and yeast. set aside for 5 minutes or until bubbly. Add yogurt, margarine, egg, herbs and set aside.

In a large mixing bowl, combine 3/4 cup all-purpose flour, 3/4 cup whole-wheat flour and salt. Blend in yogurt mixture and beat at low speed for 30 seconds. Beat 3 minutes at high speed. Stir in 1/2 cup all-purpose flour and 3/4 cup whole-wheat flour. (dough will be moist and sticky). Lightly spray a large bowl with vegetable oil. Add dough and turn once to coat evenly. Cover with towel and let rise 1-1/2 hours. Punch dough down and form into 18 balls. Lightly spray a 9x13 inch pan with vegetable oil. Arrange balls of dough in pan. Let rise 40 minutes. Preheat oven to 400 degrees. Bake rolls for 15 minutes.

Soups

Lentil Soup

1 tablespoon acceptable margarine
1 onion, chopped
2 cloves garlic, finely chopped
1 cup lentils
7 cups water
1/8 teaspoon cinnamon
1/4 teaspoon ground ginger
1/4 teaspoon cloves
1/8 teaspoon cayenne
1-1/2 teaspoons cumin
Fresh ground black pepper

In a large pot, melt margarine. Add onion and garlic and sauté until soft. Add remaining ingredients. Bring to boil, reduce heat and simmer 1-1/2 hours. Place mixture in a blender and mix well. Serve hot.

Mexican Chicken Soup

2 cups dried pinto beans
  or garbanzos
Water
1 (3 pound) frying chicken,
  skinned and all visible
  fat removed. .
(cut chicken into serving pieces)

2 cups canned no-salt added
  tomatoes
1 clove garlic, minced
1/2 cup chopped onion
2/3 cup canned mildly hot Cali-
  fornia chili peppers, diced
16 corn tortillas

Rinse and soak beans overnight. Drain; add fresh water to beans and cook according to pkg. instructions. Omit salt. Rinse chicken and pat dry. Place chicken pieces in a large pot, adding enough water to cover. Bring to a boil over medium-high heat. Reduce heat. Simmer about 25 minutes or until chicken is tender. Remove chicken pieces from broth and remove chicken meat from bones. Return meat to broth along with tomatoes, garlic, onion, chili peppers and beans. Simmer about 15 minutes. Transfer soup to individual bowls. Serve 2 corn tortillas alongside each.

Vegetable Soup

2 cups peeled, diced potatoes
1 cup diced carrots
1 cup diced celery
1 cup chopped onion
3 cups shredded cabbage
1 (6 ounce can) no salt added
  tomato paste

1 teaspoon thyme
1/4 teaspoon fresh ground
  black pepper
6 cups beef broth, low sodium
1/3 cup finely chopped
  fresh parsley

Combine all ingredients except parsley in a large stockpot. Bring to boil, reduce heat and simmer 20 minutes or until vegetables are tender. Remove 3 cups vegetables and broth and puree in blender. Return puree to pot, add parsley and reheat. Serve hot.

Fish and Seafood

Flounder Fillets in Foil

4 (5 ounce) flounder fillets
1 tablespoon acceptable margarine
1 tablespoon chopped shallots or green onions
1/2 pound mushrooms, chopped
3 tablespoons dry white wine
1 tablespoon fresh lemon juice
1 tablespoon chopped fresh parsley
Vegetable spray
1/2 teaspoon freshly ground black pepper

Rinse fish and pat dry. Set aside. To make a mushroom sauce, begin by lightly spraying a non-stick skillet with vegetable oil. Place over medium-high heat. Add margarine, shallots or green onions and sauté until soft. Add mushrooms and cook until most of the liquid evaporates. Preheat oven to 400 degrees. Lightly spray 4 pieces of heavy duty foil with vegetable oil. Place a fillet on each piece of foil; season with pepper. Spoon mushroom sauce evenly over each piece of fish. Draw edges of foil together and seal. Bake 20 minutes, or until fish flakes. Serve in foil.

Haddock with Tomatoes and Ginger

1-1/2 pounds haddock fillets
3 tablespoons flour
Dash white pepper
2-1/2 tablespoons acceptable vegetable oil
1 tablespoon grated fresh ginger
2 cloves garlic, minced
2 cups seeded, chopped tomatoes
1/3 cup sliced green onions
1 cup orange juice
1/2 cup white wine
2 tablespoons light soy sauce
1-1/2 tablespoons cornstarch
1 tablespoon finely chopped fresh parsley

Preheat oven to 350 degrees. Lightly coat a baking dish with vegetable oil spray. Rinse fish and pat dry. Set aside. Combine flour and pepper in a shallow bowl. Add fillets, one at a time, and turn to coat well. In a medium non-stick skillet over medium-high heat. Heat oil and brown fillets. Transfer them to prepared baking dish and cook 10-15 minutes.

Hearty Halibut

2 pounds halibut or other firm fish steaks
2/3 cup thinly sliced onion
1-1/2 cups sliced fresh mushrooms
1/3 cup chopped tomato
1/4 cup chopped bell pepper
1/4 cup chopped fresh parsley
3 tablespoons chopped pimento
1/2 cup dry white wine
2 tablespoons fresh lemon juice
1/4 teaspoon dill weed
Fresh ground pepper
Vegetable oil spray
8 lemon wedges

Preheat oven to 350 degrees. Lightly spray a covered baking dish with vegetable oil. Rinse fish and pat dry. Arrange onion slices in the bottom of prepared baking dish. Place fish on top. Set aside. In a bowl, combine remaining vegetables. Stir to mix well, and spread over fillets. In a small bowl, combine wine, lemon juice, dill and black pepper. Pour over fish and vegetables. Cover and bake 25 to 30 minutes or until fish flakes easily when tested with a fork. Garnish with lemon slices.

Chicken

Crispy Baked Chicken

1 (2-1/2 -3 pound) frying chicken, cut into serving pieces
1 cup skim milk
1 cup cornflake crumbs
1 teaspoon rosemary
1/2 teaspoon fresh ground pepper
Vegetable oil spray

Preheat oven to 400 degrees. Line a baking pan with foil and lightly spray foil with vegetable oil. Rinse chicken and pat dry. Set aside. Pour milk into shallow bowl. Combine cornflake crumbs, rosemary and pepper in another shallow bowl. Dip chicken pieces first into milk and then into crumb mixture. Allow to stand briefly so coating will stick. Arrange chicken in prepared pan so pieces do not touch. Bake 45 minutes or until done. Crumbs will form a crisp "skin".

Grilled Spicy Chicken Breast Fillets

1 small clove garlic, crushed
1 small onion, finely chopped
1-2 tablespoons finely chopped cilantro
2-3 tablespoons fresh lime juice
2 tablespoons olive oil
1/2 teaspoon chili powder
Fresh ground pepper
8 chicken breasts, boneless, and skinless

In a small bowl combine first seven ingredients. Mix well. Set aside. Rinse chicken and pat dry. Place in shallow glass dish. Add lime juice mixture and stir to coat chicken pieces thoroughly. Cover dish and refrigerate 2-3 hours. Stir several times while marinating to keep chicken well coated. On a preheated outdoor grill or broiler, cook marinated chicken, turning once, 6-7 minutes or until done. Serve hot.

Turkey Lasagna

1/2 cup chopped onion
1 cup fresh mushrooms, sliced
3 cloves garlic, minced
1 pound freshly ground turkey, skin removed
3 cups no-salt added tomato sauce
2 teaspoons basil
1/2 teaspoon oregano
Fresh ground black pepper
1 (10 ounce package) frozen, no-salt added, chopped spinach, defrosted
  and squeezed dry.
2 cups low-fat cottage cheese
Dash of nutmeg
1 (8 ounce package) part-skim mozzarella cheese, grated
Vegetable oil spray

Preheat oven to 375 degrees. Lightly spray a 9x13 inch baking dish with vegetable oil. In a nonstick skillet over medium-high heat, combine onion, mushrooms, garlic, and ground turkey. Sauté until turkey is no longer pink. Cover pan and continue to cook until mushrooms have released juices, then uncover and evaporate juices over high heat. Add tomato sauce, basil, oregano and pepper. Reduce heat. In a bowl, stir spinach, cottage cheese and nutmeg together well. Set aside. Lay one-third of noodles on bottom of dish; add one-half of spinach mixture, one-third of tomato sauce and one-third of cheese. Repeat layers once. Finish with one layer noodles, one third sauce, and remaining cheese. Cover with aluminum foil and bake 35 to 40 minutes.

Meats

Macaroni Beef Skillet

1 (8 ounce package) uncooked rotini pasta
1/2 pound uncooked ground round
1 cup chopped onion
3 cloves garlic, minced
1-1/2 teaspoons Italian herb seasoning
1-1/2 teaspoons basil
1 (8 ounce package) fresh mushrooms
1 (6 ounce can) no-salt added tomato paste
1 cup water
1 teaspoon Worcestershire sauce
1/4 teaspoon salt
2 tablespoons grated Parmesan cheese
2 tablespoons finely chopped parsley

Cook pasta according to pkg. directions, omitting salt, and set aside. Wipe mushrooms with a clean, damp cloth. Slice and set aside. Place beef, onion, garlic, herbs and mushrooms in a skillet. Cover and cook over medium heat, stirring occasionally, 8-10 minutes or until mushrooms have released all their juices and are fully cooked. In a small bowl, whisk together tomato paste, water, Worcestershire sauce, salt, cheese and parsley. Add to skillet. Add pasta to skillet and heat thoroughly before serving.

Bayou Red Beans and Rice

1 pound dried red kidney beans (2-1/2 cups)
1 ham bone
1 cup chopped fresh low-fat ham
1 large onion, chopped
2 stalks celery with leaves, chopped
2 teaspoons hot pepper sauce
1-1/2 cups uncooked white rice

Rinse and pick over beans. Place beans and 4 cups water in a glass bowl and soak overnight. Drain and rinse beans, then place in a large heavy pan, stockpot or Dutch oven. Add 4 cups fresh water and remaining ingredients, except rice. Bring to a boil over medium-high heat. Reduce heat and simmer 3 hours, or until beans are tender. Add water as necessary during cooking. Water should barely cover beans at end of cooking time. Prepare rice according to pkg. directions, omitting salt, and butter. Remove ham bone and 1 cup of beans from mixture. Place the reserved cup of beans in a blender. Blend until beans are mashed to a paste. Return mashed beans to mixture in pan. cut meat from bone and return to beans. Stir until thick. Divide rice equally into eight individual bowls and top with equal amounts of the bean mixture.

Braised Sirloin Tips

1/2 teaspoon freshly ground black pepper
1/2 teaspoon unseasoned meat tenderizer
2 pounds beef sirloin tips, fat removed, and cut into cubes
2 cloves garlic, finely minced
1-1/4 cups low sodium beef broth
1/3 cup dry white wine
1 tablespoon light soy sauce
2 tablespoons cornstarch
1/4 cup cold water
1/4 cup minced fresh parsley

Place a large, non-stick skillet over medium-high temperature. Sprinkle pepper and meat tenderizer on meat. Brown meat on all sides, turning often. Add garlic and onions and cook until onions are translucent. Add broth, wine and soy sauce and heat to boiling. Reduce heat, cover and simmer 1-1/2 hours, or until meat is tender.

Vegetarian

Stuffed Acorn Squash

3 small acorn squash
1 cup cooked rice
1 cup herb-seasoned stuffing mix (crumb style)
1/2 cup finely chopped onion
1/2 cup low-sodium chicken broth
1/4 cup raisins
1/3 cup unsalted dry-roasted walnuts
1/4 teaspoon freshly ground black pepper

Preheat oven to 400 degrees. Cut each squash in half and spoon out seeds. Set aside. In a bowl, combine all ingredients except squash. Fill squash halves in a 9x13 inch pan and cover with foil. Bake 1-1/4 hours or until squash is tender when pierced with the tip of a knife. Serve hot.

Stuffed Peppers

3 tablespoons acceptable vegetable oil
2 onions, sliced
2 cloves garlic, minced
1 medium zucchini, chopped
4 medium tomatoes, chopped
2 cups cooked brown rice
1/2 cup grated low-fat cheddar cheese
4 large green bell peppers
2 cups no-salt added tomato juice

Preheat oven to 375 degrees. Rinse bell peppers, cut off tops and remove seeds. Reserve hollow peppers and tops. Heat oil in large skillet over medium heat. Add onions, garlic, zucchini and tomatoes. Sauté until zucchini is tender-crisp. Do not overcook. Set aside. In a bowl, combine rice and cheese. Add to mixture in skillet and toss gently to mix well. Set aside. Pour tomato juice into bottom of a casserole dish. Set aside. Stuff peppers with vegetable mixture and replace pepper top. Place stuffed peppers in casserole. Bake 1/2 hour.

Pasta Primavera

1 cup low-fat cottage cheese
1 tablespoon fresh lemon juice
1 (8 ounce package) thin spaghetti
1 tablespoon acceptable vegetable oil
1/4 cup chopped scallions
1/2 cup chopped onion
1 clove garlic, minced
1/4 teaspoon freshly ground pepper
2 cups sliced fresh mushroom
1 cup sliced green bell pepper
1-1/2 cups sliced carrots
1 (10 ounce package) frozen no-salt added broccoli, steamed

Drain any liquid off cottage cheese. In a bowl, combine cottage cheese and lemon juice. Set aside. Prepare spaghetti according to pkg. directions, omitting salt. Drain thoroughly. Meanwhile, heat oil in skillet over medium-high heat. Add scallions, onions, garlic and black pepper and sauté 1 minute. Add mushrooms and stir 1 minute. Add bell peppers, carrots and broccoli and stir for another 3-4 minutes. Set aside. In another bowl, toss spaghetti and cottage cheese mixture to coat evenly. Top with sautéed vegetables.

$\mathcal{D}$esserts

Frozen Banana Orange Push-Ups

2 bananas
1 (6 ounce can) frozen orange juice, concentrate, thawed
1/2 cup nonfat dry milk
1/2 cup water
1 cup plain nonfat yogurt

Peel and slice bananas in a blender or the work bowl of a food processor fitted with a metal blade. Add remaining ingredients. Cover and process until foamy. Pour evenly into 6 small paper cups. Freeze. To eat, squeeze bottom of cup.

Baked Ginger Snaps

8 pear halves, canned, and in natural juices
1/2 cup firmly packed brown sugar
1 teaspoon fresh lemon juice
1/2 teaspoon ground ginger, or chopped crystallized ginger to taste
1/4 cup unsalted dry-roasted chopped pecans

Preheat oven to 350 degrees. Drain pears, reserving juice. Arrange pears halves close together in a baking dish cut side up. Set aside. In a small bowl, combine brown sugar, lemon juice, ginger and pecans; mix well. Spoon into pear halves and sprinkle with ginger. Pour reserved pear juice around pears to cover bottom of dish. Bake 15-20 minutes.

Index

D

E

M

O

T

New Titles & Bestsellers from Cathedral Foundation Press

Spiritual Living in Secular Society

The Teachings of Archbishop William D. Borders

A great man and teacher shares his vision of Catholic faith and living. 192 pp., $24 (hc) or $16 (pbk).

A Taste of Catholicism

Recipes for the Body and Soul

Over 200 recipes showcasing the archdiocese's ethnic diversity. Spiral-bound, 240 pp., $15 (pbk).

Stops Along the Country Road

Fr. Joseph Breighner

Based on Father Joe's popular radio show! 220 pp., $18.95 (pbk).

Radiant

Prayer/Poems

Diane Scharper

For grieving and bereaved seeking understanding. Over 50 poems and two prose introductions. 104 pp., $12.95 (pbk).

The I of the Beholder

Stephen Vicchio

"(There is) no higher praise than to compare Vicchio's expression to Loren Eiseley and Annie Dillard at their best."

St. Anthony Messenger

256 pp., $16.95 (pbk).

Also by "Father Joe"

A Year of Wit, Wisdom & Warmth

Collection of popular columnist's Catholic Review articles. 200 pp., $16.95 (pbk).

When Life Doesn't Make Sense

Fr. Joseph Breighner

His third and newest book looks at life, love and loss.

The Papal Visit

Beautiful coffee table book of pictures that highlights the Pope's visit to Baltimore in 1995.

144 pp., over 200 photos, $30 (hc) or $20 (pbk).

ORDER FORM

QTY	TITLE	TOTAL
_____	Spiritual Living (hc) $24	_____
_____	Spiritual Living (pbk) $16	_____
_____	A Taste of Catholicism $15	_____
_____	Stops Along the Country Road $18.95	_____
_____	Radiant: Prayer/Poems $12.95	_____
_____	The I of the Beholder $16.95	_____
_____	A Year of Wit, Wisdom & Warmth (book) $16.95	_____
_____	Words of Wit, Wisdom & Warmth (tape) $10	_____
_____	When Life Doesn't Make Sense $12	_____
_____	The Papal Visit (hc) $30	_____
_____	The Papal Visit (pbk) $20	_____

Subtotal _____

Shipping & Handling ($3.00 for first book, $.50 for each add. book) _____

Total $ _____

(All Orders Must Be Prepaid)

Payment Options ❑ Check ❑ Visa ❑ M/C ❑ Discover

Card #_____ Exp Date_____

Signature _____

Name _____

Address _____

City/State/Zip _____

Phone # _____

Mail Your Order To:
Cathedral Foundation Press
P.O. Box 777
Baltimore, Maryland 21203
FAX Orders to: (410) 332-1069 • **Phone Orders:** (410) 547-5324